you know you're in
massachusetts when...

Some Other Books in the Series

You Know You're in Arizona When . . .

You Know You're in Florida When . . .

You Know You're in Illinois When . . .

You Know You're in Kansas When . . .

You Know You're in Michigan When . . .

You Know You're in Minnesota When . . .

You Know You're in New Hampshire When . . .

You Know You're in New Jersey When . . .

You Know You're in Rhode Island When . . .

You Know You're in Texas When . . .

You Know You're In Series

you know you're in
massachusetts when...

101 quintessential places, people, events, customs, lingo, and eats of the bay state

Patricia Harris and David Lyon

INSIDERS' GUIDE®

GUILFORD, CONNECTICUT
AN IMPRINT OF THE GLOBE PEQUOT PRESS

INSIDERS' GUIDE®

Copyright © 2007 by Morris Book Publishing, LLC

Text design by Linda R. Loiewski
Illustrations by Sue Mattero

Library of Congress Cataloging-in-Publication Data
Harris, Patricia, 1949-
    You know you're in Massachusetts when— : 101 quintessential places, people, events, customs, lingo, and eats of the Bay State / Patricia Harris and David Lyon. — 1st ed.
        p. cm. — (You know you're in series)
    Includes index.
    ISBN-13: 978-0-7627-4132-8
    ISBN-10: 0-7627-4132-5
    1. Massachusetts—Miscellanea. 2. Massachusetts—Description and travel—Miscellanea.
I. Lyon, David, 1949- II. Title.
    F64.6.H37 2006
    974.4—dc22
                                                                                    2006020812

Manufactured in the United States of America
First Edition/First Printing

To the 6,349,097 reasons why Massachusetts is unique.

about the authors

Patricia Harris and David Lyon are not natives of Massachusetts but embraced the Bay State in the formative years of their higher education—his at the state university, hers at Harvard. Pat's chief claim to fame, however, was that she was standing in line the day Steve's Ice Cream opened in 1973, and David has been known to reel in codfish from the offshore banks. They are the authors of a host of magazine articles, Web essays, newspaper features, and other books about the Bay State, including *The Food Lover's Guide to Massachusetts* and *Boston Off the Beaten Path*. Pat and David can be spotted walking the streets of Cambridge, where they dwell in the strivers' ZIP code of 02139.

to the reader

It's easy to assume that American history class taught you everything you need to know about Massachusetts, but we hope you'll get to know us a little better. A lot has happened around here since some of the guys dumped tea in the harbor. And even though we're knee-deep in universities, we're not such a tweedy bunch, really. We're more likely to be reading a Spenser novel than Samuel Eliot Morison's naval history, or charting the batting average of the new outfielder at Fenway than arguing the semiotics of architectural modernism.

You don't have to scratch far below the surface to discover a sense of whimsy. Massachusetts is the land of the frappe and the imaginary scrod, giant pumpkins and magic tricks. We may be the birthplace of basketball, but we've perfected baseball martyrdom. Massachusetts is where a day at the beach means a 40-mile stretch of fine sand and big rollers, where getting a piece of pie takes the cake, and where Heartbreak Hill looms for us all.

Whether you're a new resident, a visitor, or a blue-blooded Bay Stater, we sincerely hope that this compilation gives you a handle on the strange, diverse, and ultimately charming aspects of our state.

you know you're in
massachusetts when...
...your ZIP code makes all the difference

Beverly Hills, California, might have the most famous ZIP code (90210), but 02138—just one slice of Cambridge—is one of the most influential. It's not the most expensive or the wealthiest place in Massachusetts, but it's the one that makes advertisers and opinion-makers sit up and take notice.

When the U.S. Postal Service introduced ZIP codes in 1963, the planners probably didn't realize how apt the acronym for "Zone Improvement Plan" might become. City planners and real estate agents alike find that the combination of ZIP codes and federal Census tracts yields valuable information about income, ethnicity, and education.

The ZIP code system has established a life of its own, making it a meme (an idea, value, or pattern of behavior passed down culturally, rather than genetically, through the generations). If that sounds confusing, ask someone in 02138 to explain it. The upshot is that people who live in the 2.8 square miles of that ZIP code get a much better class of junk mail.

Roughly a quarter of the houses are valued at more than $1 million—though nearby Beacon Hill in Boston (02114) tops Massachusetts ZIPs with a median house price of $1,135,000, so money isn't everything. Maybe more to the point, 02138 is the home of Harvard University, Harvard Square, and an awful lot of Harvard faculty,

02138:

Home to Harvard faculty and many of the university's most successful graduates, the ZIP code carries a distinction no other Massachusetts address can match.

senior staff, and successful alumni. These are the people who run the universe (just ask them). In 2006 some of them even launched a magazine about themselves called, natch, 02138.

This preternatural fascination with the Harvard ZIP—bred in no small part by direct-mail advertisers looking for consumers of luxury goods and contributors to political campaigns—does not extend to the adjoining neighborhoods, such as 02139 (Central Square) or 02141 (Porter Square). If an address in 02138 means having it made, then the rest of the people in Cambridge must just be strivers.

Basketball players might be getting taller every year, but this is ridiculous. A nine-story, 240-foot fiberglass sphere is the icon of the Naismith Memorial Basketball Hall of Fame and Museum in Springfield. On second thought, maybe it's not such a stretch, given what a big deal the hoop game has become.

The facility honors the memory of Dr. James Naismith. Back in 1891, Naismith nailed a couple of peach baskets to the Springfield YMCA gym walls, grabbed an old soccer ball, and invented the game of basketball. By 1892, rules had been published for Naismith's "athletic distraction," and even in those pre-Title IX times, Smith College women had organized a team by the following year. The rest, as they say, is history.

At the Hall of Fame today, adult visitors like to reminisce about the historic games that play constantly on big monitors, or comb through the Hall for their favorite professional and college players (both men and women) from the late 19th century to the present. Glass cases sketch the careers with a handful of artifacts: a size-18 sneaker, bright jerseys, autographed game balls.

The Hall of Fame is also a mecca for kids who want to chase their own hoop dreams. On the second level, diagnostic stations enable aspiring players to measure their "wingspan," gauge their reaction time,

practice rebounding skills, and learn how high they can jump—and how to jump higher. Some of the exhibits allow visitors to actually experience history. It turns out that tossing a soccer ball into a peach basket is hardly a cinch. No wonder Naismith's first game ended with the score 1–0.

The centerpiece of the 80,000-square-foot structure is, naturally enough, a basketball court, where the museum puts on weekend and school-vacation clinics and visitors are welcome to shoot some hoops. The Basketball Hall of Fame is located at 1000 West Columbus Avenue in Springfield. For information, call (413) 781–6500 or (877) 4HOOPLA or visit www.hoophall.com.

Basketball Hall of Fame:

This gleaming facility in Springfield honors James Naismith, who used peach baskets and a soccer ball to invent what would become the modern game of basketball.

Memories have a way of flooding back in Fall River, where the world's largest collection of naval war vessels fills Battleship Cove in Mount Hope Bay. The best way to tour one of these ships is with a volunteer guide who served aboard a warship. Failing that, try to tag along behind a veteran who reminisces about the difficulties of turning over in the narrow cots or of drinking coffee in the cramped mess hall. It adds a personal touch to these floating pieces of history.

The USS *Massachusetts,* the state's official memorial to World War II and the Persian Gulf War, looms largest. Built in nearby Quincy, the *Massachusetts* was the first American battleship commissioned after Pearl Harbor. She fought 35 battles, taking down 5 enemy ships and 39 aircraft. Of the 2,300 sailors who served aboard, not one died in battle.

Two PT boats—small, swift unarmored torpedo boats of the type commanded by John F. Kennedy in World War II—sit on blocks in a Quonset hut. Along with the memorabilia of the National PT Boat Museum aboard the *Massachusetts,* they constitute the largest existing collection of PT boat artifacts.

Nestled next to the high decks of the battleship is the only Gearing-class destroyer open to the public—the USS *Joseph P. Kennedy Jr.,* named after the president's brother. She was the only American vessel

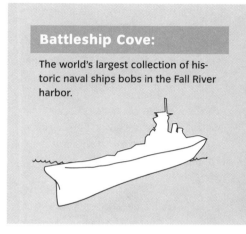

Battleship Cove:

The world's largest collection of historic naval ships bobs in the Fall River harbor.

whose crew boarded a Soviet-chartered ship during the 1962 Cuban missile crisis. Today she serves as the state's official memorial to the Korean and Vietnam Wars. Peace makes peculiar berthmates: Next to the destroyer bobs the *Hiddensee,* the only Russian missile corvette on display in the world.

A reminder of simpler times perches on a bluff above the cove. Inside a Victorian-style hippodrome, 48 carved and painted horses and two chariots whirl around on a restored 1920 Philadelphia Toboggan Company carousel. Each revolution provides a panoramic view of the fleet.

Battleship Cove is at 5 Water Street, Fall River; the carousel is located at 1 Central Street. For more information, call (508) 678–1100 or visit www.battleshipcove.org.

you know you're in
massachusetts when...
...all the king's men are put to rout

It was the Big Bang of American history—that exchange of gunfire between British soldiers and American colonial militia and minutemen on April 19, 1775. Writing generations later in his poem "Concord Hymn," Ralph Waldo Emerson dubbed it "the shot heard 'round the world." It's reenacted every year in Massachusetts on Patriot's Day (which has nothing to do, for a change, with the region's professional football team).

The 990-acre Minute Man National Historical Park helps maintain some of the historic sites and interpret the events of long ago. And each April, a column of British redcoats marches in the cold predawn mist to Lexington Battle Green to meet a company of colonial militia. No one gives an order to fire, but the hammers go down, steel strikes flint, sparks set powder burning, and blasts of fire shoot from the barrels of muskets. When the smoke clears, the colonials haul their "dead and wounded" from the field and the British, stiff upper lips and all, march onward to Concord. Hundreds of people ringing the green applaud and head off to a pancake breakfast.

The reenactment at North Bridge in Concord takes a different tone. A well-ordered band of minutemen unsettles three companies of British soldiers and then comes marching across the bridge as the redcoats

Battles of Lexington and Concord:

Each April, minutemen and redcoats reenact the opening salvos of the Revolutionary War.

are put to rout. (The fife and drum often play "Yankee Doodle Dandy.") As the real British did in 1775, the reenactors retreat with increasing alarm and anarchy, and a running battle ensues that chases the king's men back to their Boston garrison. Depending on how many reenactors are available, some of the Battle Road skirmishes also may be depicted.

For more information on visiting the battle sites, call the Minute Man National Historical Park at (978) 369–6993 or visit www.nps.gov/mima.

Whoever said "life's a beach" got it backwards for Cape Cod, where the beach is a way of life. When Congress authorized the Cape Cod National Seashore in 1961, the main objective was to preserve and conserve the tract of beach that extends almost unbroken from Nauset spit north to the tip of Cape Cod. Recreation was almost an afterthought (but what an afterthought it's been!).

A complex of town, state, federal, and private land makes up the fifth most visited park in the National Park system. It houses a far broader range of environments than the term *seashore* might suggest: extended mats of salt marsh, calm and deep kettle ponds, brooks that trickle through hardwood forest, and swamplands full of white cedar and Norway maple.

Birders flock to the National Seashore to observe the migrating warblers in the fall, nesting plovers in the spring, and rarely seen offshore species in the winter. Seal watchers marvel over the spectacle of thousands of harbor seals basking on the sand banks. And would-be whale watchers discover that they can stand at the Province Lands Visitors Center with binoculars and spy humpbacks feeding just offshore where the continental shelf drops off to deep waters.

But the richness of wildlife-watching on the National Seashore doesn't mean you can't simply enjoy the beach. Make a day of it, starting with sunrise at Head of the Meadows Beach. Next, ride the rollers on a surfboard at Nauset Light Beach (an image of the namesake lighthouse appears on countless potato chip bags). Then kayak the back side of Coast Guard Beach in the shallow waters of Nauset Marsh and marvel over the "walking" dunes of the Province Lands. From Race Point the sun seems to set over Cape Cod Bay with an almost audible hiss.

The Salt Pond Visitors Center of the Cape Cod National Seashore is on Route 6 in Eastham. For more information, call (508) 255–3421 or visit www.nps.gov/caco.

Beach:

The Cape Cod National Seashore encompasses 40 miles of sand beaches in a total area of 43,604 acres of dunes, upland forest, broad marshes, and freshwater kettle ponds.

you know you're in
massachusetts when...
...pop and jazz stars visit their alma mater

"Put your hands together, ladies and gentlemen, and give it up for Berklee's own . . ."

Sometimes confused with the sound-alike Bay Area campus of the University of California, Boston's Berklee is the premier independent music college in the world. It's one of few such institutions where the founding philosophy focuses on contemporary music and the curriculum is geared toward grooming successful performers.

The alumni list of the college, which was founded in 1945, reads like a long list of Grammy Award nominees. Although Berklee is known for its rock curriculum—it was the first school to offer an electric-guitar major—and for some of its jazz innovators, the performers who honed their chops in Berklee's classrooms, performance halls, and recording studios run the gamut of styles and musical genres. They include producer and arranger Quincy Jones, singer/songwriter Melissa Etheridge, *Tonight Show* bandleader Kevin Eubanks, jazz saxophonist/composer Branford Marsalis, singer/pianist Diana Krall, and Dixie Chick Natalie Maines.

Berklee's students and distinguished faculty enliven the Boston music scene, performing at the college and in dozens of clubs and nightspots around town. More than a quarter of Berklee's students come from outside the United States, which helps augment the

Berklee College of Music:

With a focus on contemporary music, this Boston institution counts Diana Krall, Quincy Jones, Melissa Etheridge, Aimee Mann, Natalie Maines, and Branford Marsalis among its alumni.

interplay of musical ideas from many different traditions. The extraordinary acoustics of the Berklee Performance Center make it a perfect mid-size venue for visiting artists as well as faculty and student concerts.

Berklee's tendrils spread through the adjacent areas of Massachusetts Avenue and the Boylston Street extension. The shops of this area are the city's best resources for musical instruments, sheet music, and commercial and noncommercial recorded music.

Berklee College of Music is at 136 Massachusetts Avenue, Boston. For more information, call (617) 747–8890 or visit www .berklee.edu.

Shades of Gulliver in Gardner! You could feel downright Lilliputian as you contemplate the Big Chair, a 20-foot, 7-inch straight-back brown Heywood-Wakefield chair erected in the middle of town in 1978.

It's just the latest in a series of Big Chairs built by the city to stake its claim of hegemony in the world of furniture manufacturing. The first artisans set up shop in 1805, and the most famous, the Heywood Brothers, in 1826. (Years later, their operation would become the firm of Heywood-Wakefield, which manufactured some of the most collectible mid-20th-century American furniture.) At the height of the industry in Gardner, its factories produced two million chairs a year.

Gardner erected its first Big Chair—a 12-foot-high Mission chair—in 1905. It followed up with another Mission chair (this one 15 feet high) in 1928 as it battled with Thomasville, North Carolina, for furniture-industry bragging rights. In 1935 Gardner mounted a 16-foot colonial-style Hitchcock chair, just to be sure it had the edge. Other communities got into the escalating Big Chair war, and Gardner was left in the dust until 1978, when its current Big Chair was briefly the world's largest. (As of 2006, a 60-foot chair in Italy held the record.)

The furniture industry hangs on in Gardner, but the glory days are best recounted in the Gardner Museum at 28 Pearl Street. Just look for the entry portico that's shaped like a chair. The building was a memorial to civic benefactor Levi Heywood, one of the chair company founders. For information, call (508) 632–3277 or visit www.the gardnermuseum.com.

Big Chair:

A furniture-making center for more than 200 years, Gardner advertises its craft with a chair more than 20 feet high.

It's the ultimate unsolved mystery. On August 4, 1892, businessman Andrew Borden and his second wife, Abby, were bludgeoned to death in their Fall River home.

A week later, police fingered Andrew's daughter Lizzie for the heinous act, still referred to by the Fall River Historical Society as the "crime of the century." Despite the gruesome details, the unusual spectacle of a proper Victorian spinster accused of murder, and unflagging media attention, Lizzie's trial lasted only about two weeks. The jury deliberated for an hour before declaring the defendant not guilty on June 20, 1893.

Alas for Lizzie, she lives on in infamy in the "40 whacks" doggerel, and her innocence remains a subject of much speculation and debate. Over the years Lizzie's supporters have suggested that the maid might have done it, or Andrew's former brother-in-law. Maybe it was an illegitimate son or the mysterious stranger that neighbors saw lurking outside. . . .

The case has been the subject of books, plays, a musical, an opera, and several television specials. The University of Massachusetts at Amherst even developed a curriculum project so that students could use the murders to "reconstruct the historical past" and "explore the evidence at hand."

There's plenty of evidence to explore. The Fall River Historical Society boasts the "world's largest collection of artifacts relating to the life and trial of Miss Lizzie A. Borden," displayed in several wooden cases. Some are best avoided by those with a sensitive disposition: a hatchet without a handle that may have been the murder weapon, police photos of the crime scene, and photos of the crushed skulls of the victims (these photos were viewed by the jury during the trial). Other curiosities include the billy club carried by the officer who arrested Lizzie and a lunch pail and stool that she used in a Taunton jail cell while awaiting trial.

Draw your own conclusions at the Fall River Historical Society at 451 Rock Street. For information, call (508) 679–1071 or visit www.lizzieborden.org.

Borden, Lizzie:

People in Fall River still debate whether this disgruntled daughter killed her father and stepmother with an axe.

Contrary to popular opinion in Hollywood, only a Kennedy (or a Shriver) speaks with the Kennedy accent. Most natives of Greater Boston speak a different dialect characterized by dropping the letter *r* when it follows a vowel. The spare *r* can be inserted into a word that seems to need one.

Hence, the seated statue at the Ivy League university in Cambridge (see page 47) memorializes John Hahvahd. The guy on horseback in Boston's Public Gahden is the country's initial president, Jahge Worshington. Please note that the short vowel *a* is broad, as in "ah," with the possible exception of "ant," which is an uninvited guest at a picnic. Your fathuh's sistuh is you-ah ahnt.

As if driving in Boston weren't confusing enough to the uninitiated, pahking is a whole other challenge. Someone who pulls the vehicle into a space might be known as a pahkah, not to be mistaken for a pahkher, which is a heavy coat worn when the weather gets wicked cold outside.

Taking public transit provides no respite because you must listen carefully to heah youah stop. The Cambridge terminus of the Green Line is pronounced Leechmeah. Between Kendall and Pahk Street, the Red Line stops at EmGeeEhsh/Mass Inaneah (Massachusetts General Hospital and the Massachusetts Eye and Ear Infirmary). For the benefit of out-of-towners from dialecti-

Boston Accent:

The key to understanding a Bostonian is to remember that the letter in the alphabet between *q* and *s* is "ah."

Wheah did ya pahk the cah?

cally challenged parts of the country (Jaw-jaw comes to mind), this stop is sometimes announced as Chahlz Street.

Keeping in mind the broad *a*, khakis are what you use to staht the cah. Things that are strange, unfamiliar, or wicked retahdid are also frequently described as bzah, as in "That tattoo on his foah-head is bzah." You'll find pickchahs all over the walls at the Gahdnah Museum, but if you're looking for pichahs, cross the Emerald Necklace to Fenway Pahk.

The accent isn't really so difficult. Even someone from Alabamer or Ahkansah can speak and be understood in Boston. Open wide and just say "ah."

Some things never go out of style. Writing in the *Atlantic Monthly* in 1860, Dr. Oliver Wendell Holmes Sr. (father of the Supreme Court justice) gave a name to Boston's founding families who had flourished and prospered greatly in the new world. The Boston Brahmins, he said, were a "harmless, inoffensive, untitled aristocracy."

Even more than 150 years later, there are plenty of Bostonians who wear the label proudly. Their "houses by Bulfinch, their monopoly on Beacon Street, their ancestral portraits and Chinese porcelains" are still very much in vogue. Just check out the antiques shops on Charles Street and the real estate listings for Beacon Hill town houses—even ones not designed by Boston's favorite Federal-era architect, Charles Bulfinch.

According to Holmes, the class was also marked by its "humanitarianism, Unitarian faith in the march of the mind, Yankee shrewdness, and New England exclusiveness." That latter attribute prompted another, less kind definition, first offered as a toast in 1910 at the decidedly un-Brahmin Holy Cross College alumni dinner:

So this is good old Boston,
The home of the bean and the cod,
Where the Lowells talk only to the Cabots,
And the Cabots talk only to God.

The clever little ditty resonated more roundly with the general public than Holmes's adulation. But it's doubtful that the Brahmins worry about such things. Thanks to the invention of the "spendthrift trust" (a financial instrument that lets less-than-frugal heirs live off the interest but not the principal of a family's wealth), the Brahmin class has persisted despite the perils of intermarriage. And they see little reason to change. In an old vaudeville joke, a woman from out of town (probably from some aspiring place like Philadelphia) asks a fine lady having tea at the Ritz where she gets her hats. The Brahmin turns, casts a cold eye, and replies, "Get our hats? My, dear, we *have* our hats."

Boston Brahmin:

Whether from ancestor worship or sheer frugality, Boston's hereditary upper crust hasn't changed styles since the days of Oliver Wendell Holmes Sr.

you know you're in
massachusetts when...
...Bruins romp in the Garden

"He takes the pass!" bellows the radio announcer. "Oooo-ooo! He shoots! He scores! Hat trick Oh-wah!" And the crowd goes wild.

The player in question, of course, is number 4, the legendary Robert G. "Bobby" Orr, one of professional hockey's first players to demonstrate the offensive potential of a defenseman. Contrary to many fans' sense of history, there was a Boston Bruins hockey team before Orr joined in 1966. The Bruins were members of the National Hockey League's "Original Six" that began play in 1924, facing off against the Chicago Blackhawks, Detroit Red Wings, New York Rangers, Toronto Maple Leafs, and Montreal Canadiens.

The Bruins took their original brown-and-gold uniforms from the signature colors of founding owner Charles Adams's grocery store chain. The team has a history nearly as hard-luck as that of the Boston Red Sox and a rival nearly as formidable as the New York Yankees. Now clad in black and gold, the Bruins often come within a game or two of winning the Stanley Cup, only to be rebuffed by the Montreal Canadiens. Neither the Bruins nor the Canadiens have had great success in recent decades (despite the new facilities in both cities), yet they rise to their best play when facing one another.

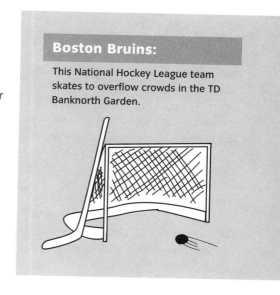

Boston Bruins:

This National Hockey League team skates to overflow crowds in the TD Banknorth Garden.

Despite the lockout of the 2004–05 season, when Bay Staters began to wonder why they had been hockey fans at all, the Boston Bruins consistently draw larger crowds at TD Banknorth Garden than their winter-sports competition, the Boston Celtics. Some pundits suggest that this is because the Bruins traditionally have been a very "physical" team, accruing many, many minutes in the penalty box. The combination of hockey's speed (a fair match for basketball) with the theatrics of professional wrestling makes a Bruins game something of a twofer.

In a city known for its Irish-American population (see page 54), it's no surprise that the charter member of the Basketball Association of America (which became the National Basketball Association) is named the Celtics. The team logo features a winking leprechaun leaning on a shillelagh and balancing a basketball on one index finger, and the team color (not colors) is Celtics green.

Note that the team's moniker is pronounced with the soft c favored by most English speakers before the recent rise of Celtic (pronounced "KELL-tik") studies. (Occasional eggheads lured to watch a basketball game have been known to let slip the academic pronunciation, to the confusion of all around them.) To confound linguistic matters, fans usually drop a syllable and refer to the team as the Celts ("Selltz"). What matters most, especially in the woefully losing era known as the 21st century, is that Boston still flies more world championship banners from its rafters than any other NBA team.

Sixteen, to be exact.

In 1995, when the Celtics had to move from the old Boston Garden to what is now known as the TD Banknorth Garden, they brought a piece of tradition with them. The Celtics are the only team in the NBA to play on a wood parquet floor. The floor consists of 247 panels, each approximately 5 by 5

Boston Celtics:

When local hoopsters hit the three-pointers, everyone in town is Irish.

feet. The panels are held together with wooden planks and brass screws—998 of them each time the floor is reassembled. (Because the Celts share the Garden with the Bruins hockey team, the parquet must be removed to install the ice.)

Famous players have come and gone over the decades, but the one man most identified with the team is the cigar-chomping Arnold "Red" Auerbach; he has served as coach, general manager, and president of the franchise. "The Celtics aren't a team," Auerbach once said. "They're a way of life." Having joined the team in 1950, Auerbach was still going strong more than a half century later.

The General Laws of Massachusetts are so succinct about the matter that it would seem to have never been in question. Part I, Title I, Chapter 2: Section 41 reads as follows: "The Boston cream pie shall be the official dessert or dessert emblem of the commonwealth."

But before the Boston cream pie achieved that status in 1996, it had to beat out venerable Indian pudding and the beloved Toll House cookie (see page 88). The Omni Parker House Hotel in Boston claims to have originated the pie, serving it since the hotel opened in 1856. Before there was a Parker House Hotel, there was already a Parker House restaurant. One Monsieur Sanzian was the French pastry chef who joined the staff in 1855. Lore in the Parker House kitchen is that Sanzian began to alter the recipe of an English cream cake, adding chocolate icing and toasted sliced almonds on top. Voilà! An American culinary heirloom was born.

Not so fast, say some American food historians. Sanzian created what is properly known as "Parker House chocolate pie" because it has a chocolate topping that differentiates it from other, earlier versions of cream cakes. Indeed, how a concoction of white cake filled with custard or pastry cream and topped with chocolate fondant icing is called a "pie" remains something of a mystery.

What made the Boston cream pie revolutionary in its day was the chocolate topping in an era when chocolate was primarily used at home, and then for beverages and puddings, not as an ingredient in restaurant pastries. But with the increasing popularity of chocolate in the 20th century, the Boston cream pie became a staple of American kitchens. Betty Crocker even offered a mix for it from 1958 into the 1990s.

Boston Cream Pie:

Layers of sponge cake with pastry cream filling and chocolate fondant icing were introduced at Boston's Parker House Hotel.

you know you're in
massachusetts when...
...lighthouse keepers are still on duty

Boston Harbor Light is the alpha and omega of American lighthouses—the first to be lit and the last remaining offshore lighthouse with a resident crew.

The first lighthouse guarding Boston Harbor was erected on Little Brewster Island in 1716 by the Colony of Massachusetts Bay. That September, it began shining its beacon to warn tall ships off the rocks. The original stone tower stood intact for another 60 years, until George Washington forced the British to withdraw their forces from Boston. On their way out the redcoats set explosives at the top of the tower with a time fuse that let them get away before it blew. Little Brewster stayed dark through the rest of the Revolutionary War, but in 1783 the Massachusetts General Court authorized a new light that incorporated the ruins of the old tower. The commonwealth operated the light until 1790, when it was turned over to the federal government.

The structure was altered over the years; it acquired heavy iron bands to stabilize it in 1809, an interior circular staircase in 1844, and another 14 feet of height in 1859. Except during the War of 1812 and World War II, when the light was extinguished to confound the enemy, it has continually served as a navigational aid.

Originally lit with tallow candles, Boston Harbor Light began burning oil lamps as early as 1789 and switched to electricity in the 20th century. With its 1859 second-order Fresnel lens and 1,500-watt electric bulb, the beam flashes once every 10 seconds and is visible for 16 miles.

Although Boston Harbor Light was automated in 1998, the light station still has a resident Coast Guard crew that records meteorological data, maintains the light, and assists with seasonal public tours. For information on tours, call (617) 223–8666 or visit www.bostonharborislands.org.

Boston Harbor Light:

The country's last remaining offshore lighthouse with a resident crew sits on Little Brewster Island in Boston Harbor.

You know it's the Sunday before the third Monday in April when every restaurant in Boston is serving up giant meals of pasta and other starchy foods for the 20,000 athletes trying to carbo-load for a grueling long-distance race the following day. Run on Patriot's Day since 1897 under the auspices of the Boston Athletic Association, the Boston Marathon is the oldest annual marathon race and one of the world's most prestigious sporting events. The list of winners in the divisions for men, women (since 1972), and wheelchair users (since 1975) reads like a roster of the United Nations.

The early Boston marathons covered 24.8 miles—the distance that Greek soldier Phidippides is said to have dashed from Marathon to Athens to announce a Greek victory over the Persian army. In 1924 Boston fell in line with the international Olympic standards by establishing the 26-mile, 385-yard course from Hopkinton to Boylston Street in Boston.

Boston has had its favorite hometown runners. John A. "The Elder" Kelley made his debut in 1928 and won the race in 1935 and 1945. His last race was at age 84 in 1992, and he still holds the record for most Boston Marathons started (61) and finished (58).

Kelley also played a role in naming one of the race's landmarks. In 1936 he caught up

Boston Marathon:

The world's oldest annual marathon kicked off in 1897.

with Ellison "Tarzan" Brown, the eventual winner, on the hills of Newton, tapping Brown on the shoulder as he passed. Brown regained the lead on the last and steepest hill, "breaking Kelley's heart," according to *Boston Globe* reporter Jerry Nason. The spot has been known as Heartbreak Hill ever since.

Runners must qualify for one of the marathon's 20,000 spots. Many of the amateur runners raise money for their favorite charities. For more information or to request an application form, call (508) 435–6905 or visit www.bostonmarathon.org.

Red Sox Nation deserved no less. After suffering decades of disappointment and humiliation, the Red Sox "reversed the curse" in record-setting style in 2004.

Boston's charter entry in the American League was a winner from the outset. Legendary pitchers Cy Young and Smokey Joe Wood led the team to the first World Series title in 1903 and four more through 1918. But then the team's owner traded star pitcher/outfielder George Herman "Babe" Ruth to the rival New York Yankees, and Red Sox fans entered an 86-year vale of tears.

Not until the 1980s did the failure of the Red Sox to win another World Series begin to achieve an aura of the supernatural. In 1986 *Boston Globe* feature writer Nathan Cobb coined the term "Red Sox Nation." Long-suffering fans embraced the term, casting themselves as baseball's equivalent of a downtrodden Balkan state steamrolled by its neighbors. At about the same time, *Globe* sportswriter Dan Shaughnessy started using the phrase "curse of the Bambino" as the only plausible explanation why the Red Sox generally led the American League in August and inevitably fell from grace (and first place) in September.

But there was finally joy in Mudville in October 2004, when the Boston Red Sox, one inning away from another wait-till-next-year winter, rallied to triumph over the pin-striped bullies of the Bronx, the New York Yankees, in the league playoffs. The comeback, to quote a *Boston Globe* editorial, "will now be the byword of hope for all teams on the brink of elimination." For the first time in 101 years of playoffs, a team down by three games had reversed fortunes to win a series in four straight. The subsequent sweep of the St. Louis Cardinals in the World Series was almost anticlimactic.

On October 27, 2004, the Red Sox had their first World Series title in 86 years, and the ghosts of the past, the Bambino included, were laid to rest.

Boston Red Sox:

In 2004 the Sox overcame the "curse of the Bambino" to win the World Series for the first time since 1918.

you know you're in
massachusetts when...
... posies span the gorge

Properly speaking, Shelburne Falls isn't a town at all, but rather a village with one foot in Shelburne, the other in Buckland, and the Deerfield River running between the two. But the siblings get along swimmingly, as they're joined by a plain iron highway bridge over the river and a far gaudier span, the village's famous Bridge of Flowers.

The latter crossing started life as a trolley bridge for the Shelburne Falls & Colrain Street Railway, which hauled freight between the textile mills of the hill village of Colrain and the railroad junction in Shelburne Falls. The trolley also carried passengers, delivering workers to the mills and enabling the hill folk to come to town to shop or go to the movies. But as more and more freight moved by truck, the trolley line went bust in 1928. At the Shelburne Falls Trolley Museum (14 Depot Street, Buckland; 413–625–9443; www.sftm.org), you can still board Car No. 10, a restored 1896 trolley car that once ran on the Street Railway line.

Since neither Buckland nor Shelburne taxpayers wanted to pony up the money to remove the trolley bridge, the Women's Club of Shelburne Falls came up with the bright idea of transforming the narrow, 400-foot-long span into a giant flower planter. More than 500 varieties of flowers, shrubs, and vines now flourish on the Bridge of

Bridge of Flowers:

This 400-foot former trolley bridge across the Deerfield River is planted with more than 500 varieties of flowers, shrubs, and vines.

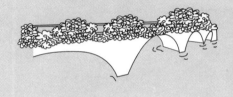

Flowers; it is in continuous bloom from the first daffodils and tulips of April to the final bright burst of chrysanthemums in October, even as the maples along the river are blazing bright red and orange. The bridge is so popular with gardeners and casual tourists alike that each year more than 24,000 visitors sign the guest book. Plantings are supported entirely by public donations and volunteer labor.

you know you're in
massachusetts when...
...old stuff is put out to pasture

Veterans of "Brimfield" have plenty of advice for newcomers to this antiques-hunting paradise: Wear comfortable shoes. Bring an umbrella. Wear sunscreen. Carry a tape measure. And, most of all, bring lots and lots of cash to increase your chances of striking a successful bargain. (No one likes to take plastic or a check.) Perhaps the best advice is that if you see a colonial boot scraper or a vintage Mickey Mouse watch that you must have, buy it on the spot. Chances are, you'll never find that dealer again.

Officially called the Brimfield Antique and Collectibles Show, this thrice-a-year outdoor emporium is the biggest of its kind in the world. More than 6,000 dealers from around the country turn out to display their wares, so it's not uncommon to see a California specialist in art pottery, a Florida dealer in antique seashell art, and/or an upstate New York shop with a great inventory of vintage Arts and Crafts furniture.

The range and quantity of goods is Brimfield's greatest appeal. Most dealers know their stuff, so it's unlikely you'll get a real steal on a Steiff teddy bear or Flow Blue soup tureen. In fact, the first Brimfield show of the year tends to set benchmarks for the ensuing summer of antiques and collectibles pricing.

Of course, you'll be rubbing elbows with (and maybe throwing elbows at) roughly

Brimfield:

In May, July, and September, thousands of antiques dealers spread their wares in the pastures of this central Massachusetts town.

130,000 other determined buyers. Each of the three shows runs for six days (Tuesday through Sunday). The selectmen of the Town of Brimfield usually authorize the sales for the weeks near Memorial Day, July 4, and Labor Day. Goods are spread out on 23 different fields that stretch roughly 1 mile along Route 20. Because not every field is open every day, many dedicated deal-seekers make their Brimfield forays a multiday affair.

One final word of advice: Bring the Ford Explorer and leave the Mini Cooper at home.

For information on the Brimfield Antique and Collectibles Show, visit www.brimfield show.com.

you know you're in
massachusetts when...
...goose bumps line the beach

What a way to start the year.

On New Year's Day the L Street Brownies don their bathing suits and funny hats, race across the sand, and plunge into the ice-cold waters of Boston Harbor. Bundled in heavy coats and gloves, their family members and friends (otherwise known as the sane ones) shake their heads, smile, and applaud. News cameras roll to capture the annual spectacle for the even-smarter folks who will watch it on TV in the comfort of their living rooms.

The earliest documented plunge was frozen in a photograph in 1904, and many believe that the Brownies are the oldest "polar bear club" in the country. The group is a fixture at the L Street Bathhouse, where they maintain their glowing tans all year by sunbathing in a sheltered area behind the building. The real gluttons for punishment even take a quick dip in the ocean a couple of times a week all winter.

Formally known as the Curley Community Center, the bathhouse is named for former Boston mayor James Michael Curley, who rewarded his working-class constituents with an extravagant "Monument to Health" during the height of the Depression. With saltwater showers, handball courts, and twin glass solariums, the facility opened in 1931 at a cost of about $400,000.

Anyone is welcome to join the hearty Brownies in their New Year's madness. Some do it as a dare. Others consider it a personal challenge. Many do it for bragging rights. Some do it because they've always done it. The Brownies point to the purported health benefits, insisting that a quick jolt in the cold water followed by a session in the bathhouse's sauna boosts the immune system's ability to fight illness.

A flu shot might be less painful.

The L Street Bathhouse is at 1663 Columbia Road in South Boston. For information on the event, which usually kicks off at 11:00 A.M., call (617) 635–5104 or visit www .lstreetcurley.com.

Brownies:

South Boston's L Street Brownies have been taking a plunge in the city waters of Boston Harbor each New Year's Day since 1904.

you know you're in
massachusetts when...
...college boys make their pitch

In an era when sports have become a high-money-stakes form of popular entertainment, the Cape Cod Baseball League seems so wholesome and pure that fans have to rub their eyes to believe it. As Christopher Price wrote in his 1998 appreciation of the league, *Baseball at the Beach,* "The Cape League remains true to the ideal of the game of baseball—that it is simply a game, to be played with nine men on a side, four bases, three outs, and a village full of people cheering for both sides."

That's pretty much what the Cape League has been since 1885, making it nearly as old as professional baseball. The 10 current teams, with such nicknames as Whitecaps, Commodores, and Gatemen, each represent a town or two. The players, by and large, are college baseball stars who come for the joy of the game, the exposure to professional scouts, and the adulation of the locals. Major League Baseball provides some money to help out the teams, but spectators are expected to toss a buck or two into the bucket to help defray costs. Players usually board with local families. Kids who bring back errant foul balls get a coupon good for an ice cream cone.

But the level of play is extremely high. One of every seven current Major League Baseball players spent at least one summer in the Cape League, making it perhaps the most productive amateur training ground for baseball players anywhere in the hemisphere. Among the alumni are Cooperstown immortals Pie Traynor, Mickey Cochrane, Carlton Fisk, Thurman Munson, and Red Rolfe.

The teams usually face off in the early evening a few times a week from mid-June until late August, when players have to pack up and head back to school. For schedules, check the sports pages of the *Cape Cod Times* or visit www.capecod baseball.org.

Cape Cod Baseball League:

One of the oldest semiprofessional summer leagues in the country is a premier showcase for college players planning to enter the professional draft.

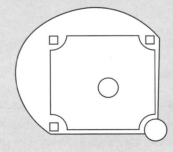

Few parts of Massachusetts are quite as directionally challenged as the Cape—which, by the way, is what all savvy residents of the state call the bent arm of land sticking out into the Atlantic Ocean. "Cape Cod" is for songwriters and people who drive up from "Lawn Guy-lund."

Newcomers to this once-remote portion of Massachusetts take a while to adjust to directions, in part because the boundaries of the sections of the Cape are so unclear. In the simplest locution, there are three segments: Upper Cape, Mid Cape, and Lower Cape. Everyone knows that Mid Cape is definitely the Town of Barnstable (which itself contains innumerable villages, most notably the pseudo-urban center of Hyannis). It probably also includes that parcel of U.S. Route 6 marked "Mid Cape Highway."

Upper Cape includes any town that borders on the Cape Cod Canal or Buzzards Bay—meaning Sandwich, Bourne, and Falmouth. Does it include Mashpee? That would depend on which real estate agent is doing the talking.

Most of Lower Cape is farther north than the Upper or Mid Cape, suggesting that it was probably named by an Australian who thinks that the South Pole should be at the top of a world map. Lower Cape definitely includes Orleans, Eastham, Wellfleet, and

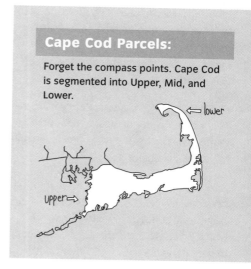

Cape Cod Parcels:

Forget the compass points. Cape Cod is segmented into Upper, Mid, and Lower.

Provincetown and might include Chatham, Brewster, and Harwich. Smart real estate agents parse the Lower Cape into "Lower" and "Outer," the latter being the portion of the Cape that might be construed on a map as the forearm, wrist, and fist of the Bay State's most confusing peninsula.

As for directions to reach or get around on The Islands (Nantucket and Martha's Vineyard), don't even ask. Just take a ferry and hope for the best.

When the Massachusetts Bay Transportation Authority introduced a "smart card" to make it easier to collect fares on its subway, bus, and trolley lines, the choice of name was obvious.

It's affectionately called the Charlie Card in honor of the system's most famous commuter, who has been riding "forever 'neath the streets of Boston."

Or at least since 1949. That's when mayoral candidate Walter O'Brien introduced a campaign song about a stranded commuter who didn't have the extra nickel he needed to get off the train. It was O'Brien's clever way of protesting subway rate hikes that required passengers to pay when they boarded and again when they exited.

Protests continue to this day, but none is as charming as the tale of the hapless Charlie ("the man who never returned") and his loyal wife, who "goes down to the Scollay Square Station every day at quarter past two, and through the open window she hands Charlie a sandwich as the train comes rumblin' through."

O'Brien lost the election, and the rates didn't go down. Today's commuters would be ecstatic to pay the Charlie-era charge of 10 cents on boarding and another nickel on exiting—amounts that could be deducted from their Charlie Cards as they wave them past electronic readers.

Charlie Card:

The once-confusing fares of Boston's subway system spawned a hit song for the Kingston Trio and a classic name for modern fare cards.

But Charlie's song (officially called "MTA") has proven as enduring as, well, fare increases—no surprise, given its folk music pedigree. It was written by Bess Hawes Lomax, a member of the famous family of folk musicologists and herself no slouch as a folklorist and guitarist. (She often performed with Pete Seeger and Woody Guthrie.) Her co-author was Jackie Steiner, a classical musician who had studied at Vassar and Radcliffe before Hawes enlisted her into the folk music movement.

The song was performed in 1950s coffeehouses and recorded by country music star Will Holt before it caught the ear of the Kingston Trio, darlings of the folk scene. Their 1959 rendition went gold and gave the catchy tune true lyric immortality.

you know you're in
massachusetts when...
...dragons dance in the streets

It takes a little detective work to identify the date for Chinese New Year. The festivities begin precisely on the first day of the First Moon of the Lunar Calendar, which usually works out to a date between late January and early February. The good news is that once the celebration starts, it stretches for 15 days—a welcome respite in the middle of a Massachusetts winter.

In Boston's Chinatown, the biggest events take place on weekends, including the annual Chinese New Year parade. The highlight is the Dragon Dance, where several dancers in a single costume snake about, rising up and bowing down. Traditional Chinese music blares, drowning out the Hong Kong pop that supplies the usual Chinatown soundtrack.

Occupying filled land between South Station and the South End, Boston's Chinatown is compact, even though it is the third largest such community in the country. Chinese began to settle in Massachusetts in the 1870s, many finding work laying the lines for Alexander Graham Bell's new telephone company, which had headquarters nearby. Although immigration from China was halted for many years, Chinatown began to grow again after World War II.

Reprising the experience of other ethnic groups, many Chinese flourished and then moved to the suburbs. Newer immigrants in Chinatown come from Southeast Asia, but the neighborhood retains a streetscape of Chinese merchants, herbalists, cultural offices, and—of course—restaurants. On weekends suburban Chinese return to the old neighborhood to buy groceries and catch up with friends over tea and dim sum.

During the fortnight-plus of Chinese New Year, Chinatown springs to life, no matter how cold the winter. Lines stretch for blocks out the door of dim sum palaces like China Pearl (9 Tyler Street, 617–426–4338), while other diners flock to noodle houses—even Vietnamese *pho* restaurants such as Hu Tieu Nam-Vang (7 Beach Street, 617–422–0501)—for long-life noodle soups. It's also good luck for a family to eat a whole, large fish, a specialty of Peach Farm Restaurant (4 Tyler Street, 617–482–3332).

Chinatown:

To celebrate Chinese New Year, dragons, lions, and other swirling figures dance down the streets of the third-largest Chinatown in the United States.

Delicious soups that incorporate mollusks from the ocean and tomatoes from the land are a staple in cuisines around the world—bouillabaisse from France, for example, or cioppino from northern California. For some tastes the list might even include a peculiar Manhattan soup with clams that some fans dignify with the name "chowder." Bostonians consider the New York version—if chilled, strained, and spiced with a dash of Tabasco—an acceptable Bloody Mary mix.

Chowder is an entirely different kettle of fish. In New England it never includes tomato—not chopped, strained, crushed, or made into a paste. The original New England clam chowder consisted of onion and salt pork sautéed together, then stewed with water, whole clams, and salt and pepper. Stale bread or crackers were stirred in to thicken the mixture. (The modern oyster cracker is a survivor of those days.) When potatoes became plentiful in the 19th century, cooks started using them to thicken *chaudiéres* (from the French word for *kettle*) right in the cauldron. New England being a dairy region, butter took the place of salt pork, and milk or cream became the primary liquid. Thus was New England clam chowder born and perfected.

Which doesn't mean chefs can't play with the flavors, as long as they don't introduce tomato. Each July since 1982, Greater Boston restaurants have vied for the title of Boston's Best Chowder. During this Harborfest event, about 12,000 very psyched chowder-lovers slurp down more than 2,000 gallons of clam chowder, tasting for subtle differences (a sprinkle of thyme, a grind of fresh black pepper, a hint of cayenne). Then they cast their votes.

A restaurant that takes top prize three times must retire to the Chowderfest Hall of Fame. As of 2006, only four had managed the feat: Turner Fisheries (Westin Copley Place, 617–424–7425), the Chart House (Long Wharf, 617–227–1576), the Mass Bay Company (Sheraton Boston Hotel, 617–236–8787), and Captain Parker's Pub (West Yarmouth, 508–771–4266).

For information about Chowderfest, call (617) 227–1528 or visit www.bostonharbor fest.com.

Chowdah:

Proper clam chowder admits to onion, butter, clams, potatoes, and milk or cream. Only Yankees fans adulterate it with tomato.

massachusetts when...

...bright light beyond the Green Monster isn't quite such a gas

Big Ben, the Eiffel Tower, the Chrysler Building, the Space Needle—every city has its defining profile in the sky. In Boston it happens to be a 60-by-60-foot piece of illuminated advertising art mounted atop a Boston University building at the edge of Kenmore Square. And every time a baseball player rockets a home run over the left field wall of Fenway Park, CITGO gets a free plug on television.

In 1965 the garish and bright CITGO sign replaced a non-illuminated sign that had been erected over a Cities Service oil company divisional office in 1940. Although some snubbed it as crassly commercial, the new sign quickly won admirers, who viewed it as an exuberant form of op art. In 1968 the short film *Go, Go CITGO* featured the sign and took honors at the Yale Film Festival. The sign was later dubbed an "objet d'heart" by *Time* magazine.

CITGO was set to tear down the sign (which was in bad condition) in 1983 when Boston preservationists rode to the rescue. Rather than let the sign be declared a landmark (which would obligate the company to keep it repaired forever), CITGO decided to light it back up before the issue could go to court. In a subsequent animated film, the sign was portrayed as "the neon god of Kenmore Square."

CITGO Sign:

This illuminated sign has shone above Kenmore Square since 1965.

Ironically, the nearly 6,000 neon tubes and 250 buzzing high-voltage transformers were all replaced in 2005 with light-emitting diodes, the little chips that make glowing digital alarm clocks possible. The newer technology consumes less than half the electricity of the old neon, yet the lights are actually brighter and the colors more intense than the original.

In one more sign of the times, the lighting sequence is computer controlled.

you know you're in
massachusetts when...
...you're warned, "Don't drive like my brother"

On Saturday mornings (and in repeats), more than four million listeners from Guam to Fort Fairfield get practical advice on automotive matters and philosophical musings about everything else from a couple of ex-grease monkeys who own a car repair shop in Somerville. Tom and Ray Magliozzi backed into this boondoggle in 1977, when local college radio station WBUR thought it would be a great idea to have a panel of car mechanics answer questions on the air. Only Tommy showed up, and when he proved a hit with both listeners, the station invited him back. The next week he brought Ray along so he'd have someone to talk to. A decade later, National Public Radio took them national.

Given NPR's reputation for highbrow, thought-provoking programming, *Car Talk* seems about as good a fit as having Susan Stamberg host a game show on Country Music Television. But as the Magliozzis point out, listeners don't have to pay to call in, and there are large stretches of the country (especially in the West) where the two choices on the radio dial are NPR or static. Also, even people who listen to NPR have cars, and fixing your car is well known to be the third-biggest technical challenge to most consumers (after getting rid of the Blue Screen of Death on the computer and figuring out how to transfer MP3 tunes to your cell phone).

Click and Clack:

Tom and Ray Magliozzi spin improbable tales and, by the way, offer advice about automotive problems nationally on *Car Talk*, which got its start on Boston's WBUR.

In addition to the radio show, Tom and Ray have figured out other painless ways to make money. They've launched a "Shameless Commerce" division on their Web site (www.cartalk.com), and they write a weekly newspaper column (under their nickname, "Click and Clack, the Tappet Brothers") that manages to answer a question or two among extended digressions on the effects of testosterone poisoning among male drivers, why women treat their cars better, and ways to help solve the energy crisis ("Convince your boss to let you work from home").

Along with the credits, each show signs off with the Magliozzis cautioning in turn, "Don't drive like my brother."

Not a chance.

If the words *summer cottage* conjure up images of a little shack by the shore where you can wander around with sandy feet, you could be in for a shock when you visit the Berkshires.

During the Gilded Age (from the end of the Civil War until the beginning of the 20th century), the notion of the "cottage" came to include a characteristically American sense of the outsized. The country's elite—merchants, tycoons, oil barons, even some of our most successful artists—built imposing mansions where they and their many best friends could spend a few weeks of the year in the only style to which they were accustomed.

The "cottages" sprouted along the seacoast—in Bar Harbor, Maine, and Newport, Rhode Island, for example—but the rolling, lush landscape of the Berkshires in western Massachusetts proved especially fertile turf for rusticating during the September and October foliage season. Ultimately, more than 100 cottages were built in or near Lenox and Stockbridge between 1860 and 1910. The advent of the federal income tax in 1913 put a damper on the indulgent lifestyle.

Often modeled on French chateaux, Italian villas, and Scottish castles, the "cottages" have been adapted to new uses. The Mount (2 Plunkett Street, Lenox; 413–637–1899; www.edithwharton.org), the 1902 home of novelist Edith Wharton, has become a museum and showpiece of Wharton's own ideas about architecture and interior decorating. Spring Lawn Mansion (70 Kemble Street, Lenox; 413–637–1199; www.shakespeare.org) now serves as a 101-seat theater for the widely acclaimed theatrical troupe Shakespeare & Company.

Blantyre (16 Blantyre Road, Lenox; 413–637–3556; www.blantyre.com), a 1901 castle complete with leaded glass windows, turrets, and gargoyles, has been transformed into one of the Berkshires' most exclusive lodgings. And the rolling green lawns of Cranwell (55 Lee Road, Lenox; 413–637–1364; www.cranwell.com) include a soothing spa adjacent to the cottage's original private golf course.

Cottages:

In the days before income tax, robber barons built their summer "cottages" in the Berkshires along the line of country house manors.

you know you're in
massachusetts when...
...beaters aren't for eggs

Who would have guessed that an intensely tart little berry that grows only in peat bogs would become the largest and most valuable agricultural crop in Massachusetts? But as new products keep hitting the shelves, from "Craisins" to "white" cranberry juice, the American cranberry remains king of the farm in the Bay State. It ranks with the Concord grape and the blueberry as one of the three commercially cultivated fruits indigenous to North America.

Native Americans harvested wild cranberry bogs for food, medicine, dye, and ceremonial uses, and the first European settlers in southeastern Massachusetts embraced the fruit from the outset. One of the earliest recorded Pilgrim recipes tells how to make cranberry sauce to accompany wild game. American whalers and China trade vessels carried barrels of cranberries on their long voyages because the berries' high vitamin C content helped avert scurvy.

Cranberries crossed the line from wild to cultivated in 1816, when North Dennis farmer Henry Hall discovered that cranberry plants covered in windblown sand grew stronger the next year, with more and larger berries. Soon farmers all over Cape Cod and Plymouth County were sanding their bogs each year and propagating plants that yielded the best harvests.

Cranberries were "dry-picked" until the 1960s, usually by laborious hand picking or raking with tined baskets. But farmers discovered that if they flooded the bogs and beat on the vines to loosen the berries, the fruit would float to the surface, where it could be vacuumed from the water. The invention of the water reel, or "beater," revolutionized the industry.

Wet-harvested berries are made into juice, jelly, jam, and dried berries. Berries sold fresh in the supermarket must still be picked dry. All the cranberries harvested in the United States in a year, if lined up side by side, would circle the globe 140 times.

Massachusetts has several local cranberry harvest festivals, the largest of which takes place in Wareham in October. For details, visit www.cranberries.org/festival/festival.html.

Cranberries:

More than a third of the world's cranberries are grown in 17,000-plus acres of bogs in Plymouth County and on Cape Cod.

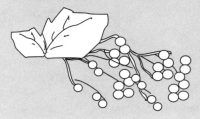

In Massachusetts the fourth Thursday of November is an annual act of cultural relativism. In other words, there are two sides to every story.

Plymouth proudly bills itself as "America's hometown," and every Thanksgiving a group of local residents dressed in Pilgrim garb marches from Plymouth Rock up to the Unitarian Church in a reenactment of the prayer service offered by half the original Pilgrim band. (The other half had not survived the first winter.) Later in the morning, another group gathers beneath the bronze statue of Wampanoag chief Massasoit. There an Indian elder puffs sacred tobacco and chants prayers before activists observe the National Day of Mourning for lost Native-American culture.

Day of Mourning:

On Thanksgiving day in the Pilgrim town of Plymouth, Native-American rights activists observe the National Day of Mourning.

The alternate Thanksgiving dates from 1970, when the Commonwealth of Massachusetts invited Wampanoag leader Frank James to deliver a speech at a public celebration. When the authorities learned that James intended to angrily denounce the nation's history of oppressing Native Americans, he was "disinvited." James delivered his speech near the Massasoit statue instead, lamenting that the harmony between Pilgrims and Wampanoags celebrated at Thanksgiving had devolved into a trammeling of Native rights.

Though the National Day of Mourning has helped focus attention on past injustices to Native peoples, it is now organized and orchestrated by a group calling itself the United American Indians of New England. The group consists largely of non-Indians, which has led the Wampanoag tribal councils of Mashpee and Aquinnah to disown the group's actions and point out that, once again, white leaders are riding roughshod over the voices and concerns of the Wampanoag nation.

you know you're in
massachusetts when...
... diners are right at home

No traveler need go hungry in Worcester, New England's second largest city and the anchor of central Massachusetts. Aficionados of roadside chow bear a special affection for the city because it was home to the Worcester Lunch Car and Carriage Manufacturing Company, one of the three major builders of diners in the first half of the 20th century. Many of the company's 651 diners constructed between 1907 and 1957 have gone to the great landfill in the sky, but 3 original Worcester diners still serve their namesake city. Waitresses with pencils tucked behind their ears are still slinging hash to cops, cab drivers, and odd-hours Edward Hopper dreamers.

The Worcester Lunch Car and Carriage Manufacturing Company, chartered in 1906 and known affectionately among diner aficionados as "Worcester Lunch," installed its first diner (with the inexplicable serial number of 200) behind Worcester's Myrtle Street post office in 1907; the company sold its last diner a half century later. It's easy to recognize a classic Worcester diner by the Gothic lettering and other premodern graphics on a porcelain enamel exterior, and by the wooden trim and wooden booths inside. The company was slow to adopt the stainless steel and streamlined designs that became more popular after World War II.

Diners:

From 1907 to 1957 the Worcester Lunch Car and Carriage Manufacturing Company produced 651 diners—3 of which are still in business in their namesake town.

The Boulevard (155 Shrewsbury Street; 508–791–4535), built in 1936, is registered as a National Historic Landmark. A bold lilluminated clock and extensive neon signage give the Boulevard the quintessential diner look. Virtually across the street, the Parkway (148 Shrewsbury Street; 508–753–9968) has been somewhat camouflaged by pebble-studded cement covering the original 1934 exterior. Known for its red-sauce Italian specials, the Parkway is a rare example of a diner without booths, just counters and stools. Holding out in the shadow of an overpass, the Miss Worcester Diner (300 Southbridge Street; 508–757–7775) looks like Dick Tracy is about to walk in, lay his fedora on the counter, and ask for "Adam and Eve on a raft."

Upon a Springfield hill, high up but quite flat
a bronze menagerie includes the Cat
in the Hat and an elephant, too.
That creature nearby is surely a Who.

This run-amok zoo fills up the Quadrangle,
where museums and a library (on an angle)
are known to Springfieldians, one and all,
as a cultural repository with nary a wall

to keep small fry from climbing about,
touching Thidwick's great rack and Horton's
      cute snout.
Indeed, there are spots worn smooth
from tiny hands, and that is the truth.

The National Memorial Sculpture Garden
is a lot to remember—really a hard one—
unless (have no fear of reprisal)
you recall that it's named after Theodor
      Geisel.

Ted was a Springfieldian lad
whose grandpa made beer and whose dad,
well, he ran the zoo. What's better to do,
if you have imagination and derring-do, too?

Ted and his folks lived out on Myrtle Street,
which as Mulberry became a peculiar treat
for a chap named Marco, who, like Ted,
thought outlandish things up in his head.

Ted oft re-created the turrets and towers
of Springfield Armory, which he studied
      for hours

and drew anew many times in his books
to amuse and delight—not just for looks.

For when Ted grew up, he moved far away
to the fantastically weird state of Californi-ay,
but he took up a pen to draw many traces
of his visually astute memories of places

on the banks of the Connecticut River
where winter makes boys and girls shiver.
He reasoned that rhymes, if fun,
might get kids to read and bask in the sun,

like the statue of Ted, at rest at his desk,
does in Springfield. You know the rest—
that this chap who replaced Mother Goose
was Theodor Geisel, aka Dr. Seuss.

The Springfield Quadrangle is located at
State and Chestnut Streets. For information
on the Dr. Seuss Memorial Sculpture Garden, call the Springfield Library and Museums Association at (413) 739–3871.

Dr. Seuss:

Life-size sculptures of
Theodor Geisel (aka Dr.
Seuss) and some of his
characters fill the
courtyard of Spring-
field's Quadrangle.

Boston often touts itself as "America's Walking City," which is a good thing, given the difficulties of driving (see page 43). The city's relatively compact size and handful of pedestrian-friendly pathways do lend themselves to getting around on foot. In fact, the Emerald Necklace is one of the best places for a leisurely stroll or a strenuous power walk. You could even say it's several of the best places.

This 5-mile swath of linked parks, ponds, and green spaces stretches from downtown Boston out through Back Bay, west through the Fens, along Muddy River through Jamaica Plain to Jamaica Pond, past the Arnold Arboretum, and out to the rolling meadows and woodlands of Roxbury/Dorchester's Franklin Park. The series of parks is definitely green, and there's no question that each piece of the chain is a gem. But that's no less than one would expect from Frederick Law Olmsted, widely considered America's first landscape architect and certainly one of the country's most influential.

Olmsted designed parks all over the country, including New York's Central Park. But Bostonians claim him as their own because he moved to the suburb of Brookline in 1883 to work on his comprehensive plan for Boston's park system. In the process, he created the world's first professional landscape design office.

He also anticipated our current preoccupation with healthy lifestyles, advocating that it was essential for mental health that people get out and enjoy "pleasing rural scenery" as a relief from the stress of urban life. His serial park, though, is just as appropriate for vigorous exercise as for meditational perambulation—witness the runners on the broad paths of Muddy River, the sailboat racers on Jamaica Pond, and the golfers at Franklin Park.

Olmsted conceived of the parks as a closed circle that would girdle the city and return to downtown, but land prices got out of hand before the city could create the final links. Cyclists doing the Tour de Emerald can reconnect to downtown by the Southwest Corridor, a relatively new sequence of parkways between the Forest Hills and Back Bay T stations.

Emerald Necklace:

This string of green parks designed by Frederick Law Olmsted connects downtown Boston with its far-flung neighborhoods.

you know you're in
massachusetts when...
...a county has its own holiday

It's time for a little history lesson before you start drinking that green beer.

In Boston March 17 is not celebrated as a holiday to commemorate the feast day of St. Patrick, the patron saint of Ireland. All those lucky public employees, teachers, and school kids have the day off to commemorate the 1776 British evacuation of Boston during the Revolutionary War.

British forces had been hunkered down in the city under a state of martial law for about nine months, but they were surrounded by colonial forces in Charlestown and Cambridge. Finally the Continental Army, under command of General George Washington, wrested Dorchester Heights from the British and fortified it with cannon that had been dragged 300 miles overland after the capture of Fort Ticonderoga. With stout British cannon aimed at his warships, British General William Howe agreed not to put Boston to the torch if his fleet of 125 ships, carrying about 9,000 soldiers and 1,000 British Loyalists, would be granted safe passage from the harbor so that they could sail to Nova Scotia.

The 215-foot-tall Dorchester Heights Monument was erected on the site of Washington's fortifications in 1898. But Boston didn't get around to declaring March 17 an official holiday until 1941. By that time Boston's large immigrant Irish population (see page 54) was concentrated in South

Evacuation Day:

Suffolk County celebrates the departure of the British occupiers from Boston in 1776—conveniently enough, on St. Patrick's Day.

Boston, practically in the shadow of the Monument, and was flexing its political muscle. Their favorite local son—James Michael Curley, otherwise known as the "Rascal King"—was in the midst of an unsuccessful campaign for his fourth term as mayor of Boston. Because the actual date of the British withdrawal from the city was in some doubt (Howe's fleet sailed away on March 26), Yankee and Irish political factions struck a compromise and named March 17 Evacuation Day.

Suffolk County, which includes Boston and some surrounding communities, marks Evacuation Day, but since the Commonwealth's government offices all have their headquarters in Boston, state employees also get the day off as a paid holiday.

massachusetts when...

... four Mannies from Madeira set a festival in motion

New Bedford may have gained worldwide fame for its exploits in the whaling trade, but it also gained a population drawn from whalers of the world. Some of the toughest and most capable came from the island of Madeira, located in the Atlantic Ocean roughly 600 miles west of its mother country, Portugal. Today, Portuguese Americans make up one of the largest ethnic enclaves in New Bedford and southeast Massachusetts. In early August each year, they throw the largest Portuguese cultural festival in the world: the Feast of the Blessed Sacrament.

Manuel d'Agrella, Manuel d'Agrella Coutinho, Manuel Sardinha Duarte, and Manuel Sebastiao Santinho survived a harrowing crossing from Madeira to the United States in 1912. To give thanks for their safe arrival, they swore to re-create their Madeiran village's *Festo de Santissimo Sacramento* in their new homeland. In 1915 they held the first religious feast.

In the decades since, it has grown into a four-day celebration of all things Portuguese. The festival attracts up to 300,000 participants for nonstop live entertainment and ethnic foods, such as *carne de espeto* (a form of barbecue) as well as stewed codfish, roasted sausages, and fresh fava beans. One recent festival managed to go through 2.5 tons of pork, nearly 2 tons of linguiça sausage, 5 tons of beef, and 400 pounds of codfish. Revelers also quaffed

Feast of the Blessed Sacrament:

New Bedford's August feast is the largest Portuguese festival in the world and the largest ethnic celebration in New England.

425 kegs of beer and 13 barrels of Madeira wine.

The festival takes place over the first full weekend in August, and admission to the grounds is always free. For more information on the festival and related Portuguese-American events in and around New Bedford, call the Clube Madeirense S.S. Sacramento at (508) 992–6911 or visit www.portuguesefeast.com. The small Museum of Madeiran Heritage sits on the feast grounds at 1 Funchal Place (508–994–2573); it is open on Sundays from April through November to show off its collection of artifacts and photographs documenting Madeiran immigration to the United States.

you know you're in
massachusetts when...
...brides-to-be storm the Basement

The first veterans of the event sometimes called the "running of the brides" have celebrated their golden anniversaries by now. Since 1947, Filene's Basement at Downtown Crossing in Boston (426 Washington Street; 617–348–7848) has enticed budget-minded brides-to-be with the chance to secure the dresses of their dreams at a discount. The store's buyers accumulate surplus wedding gowns from overstocks, cancelled boutique orders, and returns from bridal shops until a critical mass is on hand. Then the store announces a Bridal Event date on its Web site.

It is the moment that thousands of Boston-area women (and a few men) await.

Many gowns bear their original price tags (sometimes upwards of $9,000), but most are marked down to less than $500. When the doors open at 8:00 A.M., brides-to-be and their private troops storm the Basement. It usually takes less than one minute for the racks to look like a cornfield after a flock of locusts has moved through.

In a time-tested strategy, each bride grabs as many gowns as she can carry, repairs to a corner, and starts trying them on. Her entourage protects the stash, acts as instant fashion advisors, and ultimately swaps with other shoppers. The bartering of gowns is perhaps the most socially complex part of the experience, and having a good negotiator on your team could mean the difference between getting married in a Dior or a Dumpty. Smart team members wear matching jerseys or hats so the bride-to-be can spot them easily in the crowd.

Tips on the Basement's Web site help prepare shoppers for the big day. The dress code bans high heels (bad for the dresses) and flip-flops (bad for the toes in the melee) and encourages brides-to-be to wear sports bras and shorts so they can preserve their modesty while slipping into and out of gowns in the crowded aisles. The Basement also reminds participants to be considerate of others, suggesting that punching out another shopper to get a gown is likely to put a damper on any bride's wedding day.

Filene's Basement:

The offshoot of the store that pioneered the "automatic markdown" back in 1908 courts mayhem with its sales of deeply discounted wedding gowns.

you know you're in
massachusetts when...
...First Night is really first

Not to quibble, but First Night really ought to be called Last Day. Boston's celebration extraordinaire begins with family activities shortly after lunch on December 31 and doesn't end until midnight fireworks over Boston Harbor bid adieu to the old year and usher in the new.

In between, revelers of all ages peruse art exhibits and watch screenings of cutting-edge animation or the latest art films. They settle in seats for tango, ballet, and hip-hop performances or take to the dance floor to try their own salsa or swing moves. They listen to organists, classical guitarists, blues pianists, saxophone quartets, and gospel choirs. They laugh at improv and comedy routines, marvel at acrobatic troupes, and check out the poetry slam. Almost everyone lines the streets for a rollicking Mardi Gras–inspired parade at dusk.

First Night began in 1976, when a group of artists and their friends directed their creative energies to creating a new kind of New Year's Eve celebration that didn't involve too much champagne or a passel of noisemakers and funny hats. (Costumes, however, are welcome—the wilder the better.) The first modest celebration took place on Boston Common; although the festivities are still concentrated in downtown Boston and Back Bay, they've spread throughout the city to encompass more than 40 indoor and outdoor venues and involve more than 1,000 artists.

The party goes on regardless of the weather—in fact, the colder, the better for the giant ice sculptures that can weigh up to 45 tons. The sculptors work their magic on the Boston Common and on Copley Plaza, and crowds are always eager to see what they dream up each year.

The city has embraced First Night whole-heartedly. Usually about a million people join the party, though the ranks swelled to more than double that for the 2000 millennium celebration. First Night has happily spawned imitators. More than 100 cities put on their own versions of Boston's celebration on December 31.

But First Night was truly first. And, Bostonians would say, first is best. For a schedule of activities, visit www.firstnight.org.

First Night:

The original arts-oriented New Year's Eve celebration was launched in Boston in 1976.

In 1602, when the English explorer Bartholomew Gosnold was surveying the coast of what would eventually be called New England, he was particularly taken with an island he christened Martha's Vineyard. (Legend has it that he named it for his daughter and for the abundance of wild grapes there.) More specifically, he took delight in high cliffs that revealed stratified bands of colored clay. He dubbed the cliffs Gay Head.

Gosnold was hardly the first to be captivated by the formations. The Wampanoags already living on the island considered the cliffs a sacred place—Aquinnah; after the tribe gained federal recognition in 1987, the land reverted to its original name. The cliffs are an odd bit of geology. Unlike the glacial debris that makes up most of Cape Cod and its associated islands, the cliffs of Aquinnah were formed when a chunk of ancient sea floor was pushed up to the surface by a cataclysmic collision of tectonic plates. The exposed face is an open book of more than 100 million years of life on Earth.

A great band of brownish black lignite coal—the remains of plant life from the Cretaceous period (65 to 144 million years ago)—lies near the base. Eroded pieces accumulate on the beach and look like the leavings of a campfire. But the true wonders lie trapped in the colored clay

Fossils:

The brilliantly colored Aquinnah cliffs on Martha's Vineyard hold fossils that range from crabs and clams to wild horses and whales.

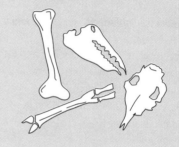

deposits, which have captured and preserved fossils of everything from extinct species of whales and giant sharks (shades of *Jaws!*) to clams, crabs, camels, and wild horses.

The cliffs have been designated a National Natural Landmark, and direct access to them is permitted only to members of the Aquinnah Wampanoag tribe. The bluff near Gay Head Light (constructed of red brick baked from the Aquinnah clay) provides the best distant view of the cliffs. Nonmembers of the tribe may park in a tribal pay lot about a mile away from the cliffs and walk along the beach at low tide for a closer look.

you know you're in
massachusetts when...
... fireworks pop after the Pops' serenade

As you cross the footbridge over Storrow Drive en route to a concert on Boston's Esplanade, say a word of thanks to Arthur Fiedler. The span under your feet was dedicated in 1953 to the legendary Boston Pops conductor who "has here brought the music of the masters to countless thousands. . . ."

The grassy Esplanade along the banks of the Charles River is an ideal place to stretch out a blanket, unpack a picnic, and listen to live music. Pop, rock, and jazz concerts are staged here all summer, but the most anticipated event of all is the Boston Pops extravaganza on July 4.

Arthur Fiedler launched free Pops concerts on the Esplanade in 1930 to share his love of music with those who might never find their way to a seat in Symphony Hall. In 1974 he teamed up with local businessman David Mugar to create a holiday concert with pizzazz. By the time Fiedler retired in 1979, the July 4 event was practically a local institution. Subsequent conductors John Williams (composer of the *Star Wars* theme) and Keith Lockhart have added their own stamp to the musical program. But woe be to anyone who messes with the evening's signature event: the playing of Tchaikovsky's *1812 Overture,* enhanced with cannon fire, pealing bells, and a few fireworks.

After the concert, the true fireworks begin as more than 10,000 shells and devices explode over the Charles River.

Fourth of July:

The eagerly anticipated Boston Pops holiday concert at the Hatch Shell on the Esplanade leads into a fireworks display that pulls out all the stops.

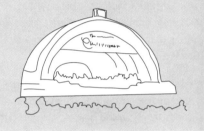

Diehard music fans are already lined up when the gate opens at 6:00 A.M. so that they can stake out a place in front of the Hatch Memorial Shell, the sound-projecting structure built in 1939 to shelter the players and enhance acoustics. The banks of the river fill throughout the day. Latecomers often station themselves on the other side of the river in Cambridge. From this vantage point, the Boston city skyline is the glittering backdrop for the fireworks display.

The event is broadcast on the CBS television network, but nothing beats being there in person. For more information, visit www.july4th.org.

James Bond might have preferred his martinis "shaken, not stirred," but in eastern Massachusetts a drink of milk, ice cream, and flavored syrup must definitely be stirred, even whirred. This is accomplished with the blades of a blender or a milk shake machine, even though the resulting beverage is by no means known as a milk *shake*. In fact, if you ask for a milk shake in many soda shops of Massachusetts, you'll get a drink of cold milk with syrup.

The ice cream drink in question is a *frappe* (rhymes with *snap*), from the French past participle *frappé* of the verb *frapper,* which means "to knock." To confuse matters all the more, in France a *frappé* is a liqueur poured over shaved ice. The "knock" part comes from the act of crushing ice by smacking a cube with a hammer or the handle of a bar knife. How this name crept into Boston argot is a mystery.

At its affiliated restaurants, Brigham's Ice Cream company (founded in 1924 in New Highlands) calls a spade a spade—or a frappe a frappe. But the treachery of geography shows up in the restaurants of the Friendly Ice Cream corporation (founded in 1935 in Springfield). Friendly's refers to a frappe as a *milk shake*. Herrell's—the relative newcomer to the Bay State ice cream industry—splits the difference. Its Cambridge store serves a frappe, while the Northampton outlet menu lists a milk shake.

Southeast Massachusetts towns near the Rhode Island border confound the issue by calling a frappe a *cabinet*. The etymology of that term supposedly can be traced to the first milk shake machines (used to make frappes), which were so messy and loud that they were enclosed in a wooden cabinet to avoid spewing the mixture all over the counter.

On second thought, make ours a martini.

Frappe:

In the Bay State, the fountain concoction containing milk, flavored syrup, and ice cream is properly known as a frappe.

you know you're in
massachusetts when...
... a red stripe runs through colonial and Federal history

The term *Cradle of Liberty* gets tossed around a lot when Boston and Philadelphia vie for historic bragging rights. The City of Brotherly Love boasts Independence Hall, centerpiece of what it calls "America's Most Historic Square Mile." In this particular Cradle of Liberty, the Declaration of Independence was first read and the new country set about making its laws.

Bostonians, on the other hand, set the Revolution in motion with their fiery rhetoric and confrontations with British soldiers. As evidence, Boston offers the Freedom Trail, a 2.5-mile path linking 16 sites that bore witness to the events of history. No other city contains so many sites with a Revolutionary pedigree. Chief among them, of course, is Boston's own Cradle of Liberty: Faneuil Hall. In the auditorium above the food market stalls, early patriots railed against British control and advocated for change.

In 1951 newspaper columnist William Schofield suggested creating a "Puritan Path" or "Loop of Liberty" to help visitors find the historic spots seemingly lost in the modern city. Within a few months someone came up with a better name, and the "Freedom Trail" was born. By 1958 red bricks and paint marked the route.

The red stripe makes navigating easy, so visitors can concentrate on soaking up some history. At the Old South Meeting House, patriots met in 1773 and decided to protest the British tea tax by throwing a cargo into Boston Harbor. Paul Revere snuck out of his North End house to embark on his famous midnight ride. Lanterns in the tower of Old North Church told him from which direction the British were arriving.

There are also many modern diversions along the Trail. Street performers hold forth outside Faneuil Hall, the anchor of Quincy Market with its food court and shops. Italian cafes along Hanover Street in the North End are perfect for a quick pick-me-up with a cannoli and an espresso.

For a map and seasonal walking tour information, stop by the Boston National Historical Park Visitor Center at 15 State Street, call (617) 242–5642, or visit www.nps.gov/bost or www.thefreedomtrail.org.

Freedom Trail:

Sixteen historic sites are linked along a red line that stretches 2.5 miles from Beacon Hill to Old Ironsides in Charlestown.

It must have been one of those *Eureka!* moments akin to Tom Edison switching on his first light bulb or Alex Bell placing the first phone call. On July 3, 1916, Lawrence "Chubby" Woodman was preparing for the Independence Day crowds at his Essex food shack by frying big vats of the potato chips for which the two-year-old establishment was locally famed. Woodman's also sold a lot of soft-shell clams in those days (as it does now), and someone suggested that Chubby drop a clam or two into the boiling oil—just to see what happened.

Gastronomic nirvana.

When Woodman's offered fried clams the next day, diners ate every batch the kitchen could make. Aficionados still line up for clams at Woodman's of Essex, the acknowledged birthplace of fried clams and one of the best places to sample them. While soft-shell clams are found from Nova Scotia south to Virginia, few environments produce quite such sweet, plump, and juicy clams as Ipswich Bay and the flats of the Essex River. This subspecies is known in the restaurant trade as the Ipswich clam—high praise for the lowly mollusk.

The true Massachusetts fried clam is never a *clam strip,* which is nothing more than a rubbery slice of sea clam. The local term for the preferred delicacy is *whole belly,* a reference to the clam body that explodes with

Fried Clams:

Lawrence "Chubby" Woodman, proprietor of Woodman's of Essex, served the first battered and deep-fried clams in 1916.

flavor when you bite into it. Fried clams must be freshly dug, dusted in a mixture of white and corn flours, then dipped in milk or buttermilk and dusted again. They must be cooked in large vats (never small frying baskets, where they would stick together) at precisely 350 degrees. Any cooler and they come out soggy with grease; any hotter and they burn.

Tartar sauce or lemon is optional.

Woodman's of Essex is located at the edge of the Essex River at 121 Main Street. It's an "eat-in-the-rough" place, which means no table service. For information, call (978) 768–6057 or visit www.woodmans.com.

you know you're in
massachusetts when...
... millions go missing

It used to be that when Boston crime aficionados got together, the conversation would invariably turn to the astonishing Brinks Job, the 1968 armored car robbery that newspapers of the era called "the crime of the century." But the Brinks theft of $2.7 million pales by comparison with the Gardner Heist.

In the wee hours of March 18, 1990, two thieves overwhelmed the guards at the Isabella Stewart Gardner Museum and made off with 13 works of art valued at the time at a cool $200 million. According to the FBI, the daring nighttime theft was the most lucrative art heist in U.S. history. More recent estimates place the value of the stolen works in excess of $300 million.

The losses included the only Vermeer in a New England collection, *The Concert,* and three Rembrandts: *A Lady and Gentleman in Black,* a self-portrait, and *The Storm on the Sea of Galilee*, the painter's only seascape. Also lost were five works by Degas, a Manet oil painting, and a Shang Dynasty bronze beaker.

Although tantalizing rumors surface periodically in the press, the $5 million reward for information leading to return of the works goes unclaimed. Boston society matron Isabella Stewart Gardner created the museum, and under the terms of her will, the collection must remain as she arranged

Gardner Museum:

This art-filled Venetian-style palazzo was the site of the most lucrative art heist in U.S. history.

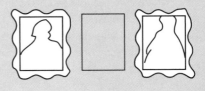

it. An explanatory note hangs next to the bare spot where each stolen work should be. Yet the riches are barely diminished. Set in the founder's Venetian-style palace, the museum retains a lush collection of more than 2,500 objects, including what many art professionals consider the single most important work of art in the city, Titian's *Europa.*

The Isabella Stewart Gardner Museum is located at 280 The Fenway, Boston. For more information, call (617) 566–1401 or visit www.gardnermuseum.org.

you know you're in
massachusetts when...
...every kind of traffic jam has a name

Boston traffic snarls are part of the city's identity. Indeed, Boston drivers take a kind of perverse pleasure in wending their way through the nastiest conditions—and a kind of perverse pride in the fact that if they can drive unscathed in Boston, they're ready for any roads in the world. (It's true.)

The training grounds for the world's most accomplished stunt commuters are a natural outgrowth of the interface between winding colonial-era streets and the great asphalt bands of superhighways. Traffic has always been so bad that the first traffic reports date from 1921, when very few Bostonians had cars—or radios, for that matter.

But Mean Joe Green of WBZ (AM 1030) and Kevin O'Keefe of WHDH (AM 850) brought traffic reporting into the modern era when they took to the air in helicopters in 1960. Green might have been the greater pilot, but O'Keefe (real name: Arthur Mctague) had the faster mouth. In effect, he created the traffic terminology that remains central to the Boston lexicon.

O'Keefe called the paltry pace of the morning commute "the snail trail" and referred to the evening exodus down the Southeast Expressway as "cram and jam." Just getting onto the Expressway was inevitably hampered by what O'Keefe dubbed "ramp cramp" (backup on the entry ramps) and

"lane sprain" (a condition caused when a lane of traffic is closed for construction). He also coined the term "bumper thumper" for the small touch-and-go accidents that happen in slow, heavy traffic.

But O'Keefe's finest contribution to the art and science of traffic reporting was his term *gawkablocka*. In a single word O'Keefe encapsulated the jam caused when motorists slow down to stare at the wreckage of a severe accident. When the Massachusetts State Police began using a roadside accident shroud, they took a leaf from O'Keefe and called it the Gawker Blocker.

Gawkablocka:

When drivers stare morbidly at an accident on the side of the road, they invariably create a block in traffic.

43

you know you're in
massachusetts when...
...drums and kettles don't make music

When you're cooling down from the August heat in a deep freshwater pond on Cape Cod or enjoying the sea breezes in a romp across the ridges of one of the Boston Harbor Islands, consider that you owe it all to the "big chill." The Laurentide ice sheet left much of what is now Massachusetts behind when it began retreating 15,000 or so years ago.

Glacier-carved landscapes are hardly unique to Massachusetts, but they dominate the geography of the Bay State. Cape Cod is all that remains of what was once a mile-thick bank of debris deposited by glacial melt-water and the bulldozing action of the ice, a so-called terminal moraine. Aerial photographs show a couple of ridges running up the spine of the Cape—places where the glacial melt paused for a thousand years or so. The islands of Martha's Vineyard and Nantucket, and even the underwater shoals off Nantucket, are similar dumps of debris.

Some of the most obvious glacial features are the Boston Harbor Islands. They consti-tute what geologists call a *swarm* of par-tially submerged drumlin hills. A drumlin is simply a teardrop-shaped hill formed by clumps of detritus from a retreating glacier. (The shape results from the sculpting effects of melting water.) During the last glaciation, so much water was locked up in the ice that Boston Harbor was dry land and the islands were little mountains.

Those cool lakes and ponds on Cape Cod—and even in Boston, in the case of Jamaica Pond—are *kettles*. When the ice receded, big chunks broke off, much as big pieces break off the modern-day glaciers in Alaska. When a large block of ice became buried in sand and dirt, it would take centuries to melt, eventually leaving behind a hole or depression in the land that would then fill with water. If the kettles were shallow—as they were in southeastern Massachusetts—the resulting pond might become a marsh and eventually a peat bog full of cranberries.

Massachusetts is the way it is because it used to be so cool.

Glacial Geology:

Many distinguishing features of the Massachusetts landscape, such as drumlin hills and kettle ponds, were formed by glaciers.

you know you're in
massachusetts when...
...flowers are fragile

Harvard University's glass flowers are unique. It took almost 50 years for two talented glass artisans to fashion these loving and accurate tributes to nature; the master crafters took the secrets of their techniques to their graves. Fortunately, the glass models are more enduring than the living specimens on which they were based.

The remarkable life-size models of 830 species range from delicate orchids to deadly Venus fly traps. They constitute the most popular exhibition in the university's Museum of Natural History. About 120,000 people a year tiptoe past the two-tiered wooden cases to marvel at the glassblowers' artistry and proclaim, "I can't believe they're not real." Botany students are sometimes found studying the magnified parts—leaf, stem, bud, blossoms, sometimes cross-sections—as they cram for exams.

Leopold Blaschka and his son Rudolph were the last in a family line of central European glassworkers that extended back to the 15th century. They were known for their amazing prosthetic eyeballs and their jewelry when the founder of Harvard's Botanical Museum (now part of the Museum of Natural History), George Lincoln Goodale, discovered them on an 1886 trip to Europe.

With funding from the Elizabeth Ware family, Goodale commissioned the Blaschkas to create life-size teaching models of botanical specimens that would be more accurate

Glass Flowers:

Visitors are admonished not to jostle the cases when they peruse the 3,000-plus models of plants created between 1887 and 1936 by German master glass artisans.

and last longer than the papier-mâché or wax models used at the time. The specimens constitute the Ware Collection of Blaschka Glass Models of Plants.

Until Leopold's death in 1895, the father-son team was able to make about 100 models a year. The first shipment to the museum (in 1887) arrived broken, but by the time Rudolph stopped working in 1936, the total number of models exceeded 3,000. Their handiwork is so detailed that even tiny hairs on pitcher plants are reproduced in exact detail. The Blaschkas even depicted flowers being pollinated and modeled fruits that had been attacked by disease.

The Museum of Natural History is on the Harvard campus in Cambridge at 26 Oxford Street. For more information, call (617) 495–3045 or visit www.hmnh.harvard.edu.

you know you're in
massachusetts when...
... your state song was written by an unreconstructed hippie

Composers can't seem to get enough of Massachusetts. The commonwealth has an official song, polka, glee club song, ode, patriotic song, and ceremonial march. But perhaps best of all is the official state folk song adopted by the legislature in July 1981. Folklorists would be hard-put to call "Massachusetts" an actual folk song, since it's hardly an anonymously authored tune with words handed down through the generations. "Massachusetts" came straight from the pen of the unreconstructed avatar of the counterculture, the bard of the Berkshires, Arlo Guthrie.

The son of singer, songwriter, and political agitator Woody Guthrie, Arlo was born in Coney Island, Brooklyn, but moved to the Berkshires in his teens and received his high school diploma from the Great Books– based private Stockbridge School. "A Thanksgiving dinner that couldn't be beat" with Ray and Alice Brock (a teacher and a librarian, respectively) formed the basis for the rambling 18-minute, 20-second "Alice's Restaurant Massacree," which launched Guthrie's performing career.

Some four decades later, Guthrie is still on the road for 10 months a year, covering the United States "from the redwood forests to the Gulf Stream waters" (as his father put it). His assertion in the state folk song that "There ain't nowhere else to be / but Massachusetts" carries the weight of experience.

Guthrie, Arlo:

Son of legendary folk singer Woody and a longtime Berkshires resident, Guthrie penned "Massachusetts," which became the state folk song in 1981.

In 1991 Guthrie purchased the former Trinity Church where the Brocks had lived and renamed it the Guthrie Center, in honor of his parents. The center operates as a not-for-profit interfaith church foundation dedicated to providing a wide range of local and international services. The center's musical performance series includes Arlo's annual benefit concert.

The Guthrie Center is located at 4 Van Deusenville Road in Great Barrington. For more information, call (413) 528–1955 or visit www.guthriecenter.org.

you know you're in
massachusetts when...
...a lying statue graces a hallowed green

Visitors to "Old" Harvard Yard inevitably gravitate to the seated statue of John Harvard in front of University Hall. Tradition has it that it's good luck to rub Harvard's toe, and few can resist the temptation to give it a quick swipe. Who knows, maybe some of Harvard's smarts will rub off, too.

Student guides like to boast that Harvard's likeness is the third-most-photographed statue in the country, after the Lincoln Memorial and the Statue of Liberty. Almost every student poses there on graduation day wearing a cap and gown and a big grin and clutching a diploma. And almost every visitor records his or her time at Harvard, however brief, by taking a photo in front of the university founder.

And that's the rub. The handsome image suffers from a lack of truth in advertising. It's popularly known as "The Statue of Three Lies" because its inscription, "John Harvard, Founder, 1638," is wrong on all counts.

First, that's not John Harvard on the pedestal. The young preacher had been dead for almost 250 years by the time the university got around to immortalizing him in bronze (in 1884)—and he had left no personal images behind. Even a master sculptor like Daniel Chester French (who later created the Lincoln Memorial in Washington, D.C.) could not create a credible likeness. Some speculate that French persuaded a popular member of the class of 1882 to serve as the model for Harvard's head.

Second, Harvard cannot properly be credited with founding the university. When he died in Charlestown in 1638, he did leave half his estate and his library to the fledgling Cambridge college that had been founded by the Massachusetts Bay Colony to educate ministers. The college honored its first benefactor by assuming his name.

Third, Harvard was founded in 1636, not 1638.

You can pick up other arcane information on the university's walking tours, which depart from Holyoke Center at 1350 Massachusetts Avenue. Call (617) 495–1573 for schedule information.

Harvard Yard:

The legend on the statue of John Harvard, centerpiece of the walled confines of the original Harvard College, famously includes three factual errors.

Most of the bright leaves of autumn have fallen to the ground when, suddenly, the Charles River between Boston and Cambridge is afloat with the hot hues of racing sculls and the basin echoes with the barks of coxswains and the heaving breaths of crews pulling in unison. For two glorious days in October, the elite speedsters of the rowing world slice through the blue river in the Head of the Charles Regatta. More than 7,000 athletes compete in what has become the largest two-day rowing event in the world.

It wasn't always the Great Race. Back in 1965 a Harvard University sculling instructor proposed a "head of the river" race on the Charles similar to those held in his native England. So-called "head" races are a class of rowing regattas that generally cover a course of 3 miles. Long boats start sequentially every 15 seconds and race against each other and the clock for honors in categories for single scullers, doubles, fours, and eights in a total of 24 different events. The winners of each race receive the honorary title of "Head of the Charles."

By 1997 the event had become so popular that organizers at the Cambridge Boat Club expanded it to two days to get in all the races without undue congestion on the river. The weekend is now a de facto world summit of sculling and crew.

Head of the Charles Regatta:

More than 7,000 athletes compete each year in the world's largest two-day rowing event, first held in 1965.

Rowers set off at the Boston University (BU) Boathouse, in the shadow of a railroad trestle and the BU Bridge. They proceed through five more triple-arch bridges to the finish line at Gerry's Landing in Cambridge, home of the Cambridge Boat Club. On any given regatta weekend, up to 300,000 spectators line the river banks and swarm those bridges, cheering and taking blurry photographs of the human equivalents of water bugs.

If you're looking to dip your own oar in the water (or just want to watch), call (617) 868–6200 for more information or visit www.hocr.org.

you know you're in
massachusetts when...
...studies get to the heart of the matter

These days contradictory studies seem to emerge every week about the health benefits of lifestyle changes. But until the Framingham Heart Study was launched in 1948, doctors didn't even talk about such things as "risk factors," a term the study coined. Data collected from residents of Framingham have led to more than 1,000 scientific papers and established many of the major risk factors associated with heart disease and stroke. Some discoveries have become so ingrained in our culture that it's hard to believe they were discoveries at all.

For example, before Framingham, doctors believed that cigarette smoking had no relation to heart attacks and stroke. They also thought that high blood pressure was a good thing in the elderly because it meant blood could get pumped to the brain through narrowed blood vessels.

The Framingham study is a marvel of simplicity. In 1948 doctors enrolled 5,209 healthy residents between the ages of 30 and 60 and began monitoring their lifestyles and giving them in-depth physical exams every two to four years. In 1971 the study recruited 5,124 children (or their spouses) of the original participants, giving the scientists a picture of heart-related lifestyles over two generations.

The beat (heart beat, that is) goes on. By following people closely over decades and examining patterns of health or disease within families, researchers have refined their findings. For example, they initially identified cholesterol as a risk factor for developing heart disease; now they are studying the unique characteristics of low-density and high-density cholesterol and are working to identify the genes that regulate how the body uses them. Verified links among exercise, diet, diabetes, and heart disease are already changing the way preventive health care is practiced. And information gathered from some of the aging original participants provides a unique window on dementia, arthritis, osteoporosis, and degenerative diseases of hearing and vision.

Investigators have plans to add a third generation of study participants in the near future.

Heart Health:

The Framingham Heart Study has revealed most of what we know about the connections between lifestyle and cardiovascular health.

you know you're in
massachusetts when...
... old apples get their dew

When Leominster-born John Chapman headed west around 1797, he took little bits of Massachusetts with him. While spreading the word of God, this itinerant preacher also spread the seeds of apples and became known as Johnny Appleseed.

Except for tart crabapples, the apple isn't native to North America, but the Bay State has always been an entry point for apple seedlings from England (such as Cox Orange Pippin and Winter Pearmain) and France (such as Pomme de Reina and Caville Blanc). It's also been a cradle for dozens of American varieties, often named for the towns where seedlings were first selected—Roxbury Russet, for example, or Westfield-Seek-No-Further.

Many of these venerable varieties have disappeared from chain grocery stores. But the state's orchardists are in the vanguard of the heirloom apple renaissance. They cultivate the old trees and their young scions in the hill country of western Massachusetts and in the Nashoba Valley of eastern Massachusetts, the country's first fruit bowl.

One key resource for this recovery is the pomological ark maintained by the Worcester County Horticultural Society at its Tower Hill Botanic Garden facility. The Davenport Collection is an orchard of 119 apple varieties that were popular in the 19th century but are not widely grown today. During the Depression, the state hired unemployed

men to root out and destroy neglected fruit trees throughout the state. Alarmed at the potential loss of great apples, S. Lothrup Davenport single-handedly saved many of them on his own orchard.

Folks in the hill country around Colrain are glad he did. Heirloom apples have been key to reviving the art of making fine ciders. Each November, enthusiasts get together to celebrate all things apple at Cider Days—one of the best chances to taste several dozen nearly extinct apple varieties.

Tower Hill Botanic Garden is located at 11 French Drive in Boylston. For more information, call (508) 869–6111 or visit www.tower hillbg.org. For information about Cider Days, call the Franklin County Chamber of Commerce at (413) 773–5463 or visit www.ciderday.org.

Heirloom Apples:

Massachusetts orchardists are among the leaders in the cultivation and promotion of pre-1900 apple varieties.

50

you know you're in
massachusetts when...
... knights are bold

The Higgins Armory Museum harks back to an era when "homeland security" meant having a wide moat around your house and a bunch of serfs to pour boiling oil on anyone who sought to breach the defenses. Yet it's a welcoming place devoted to the collection, preservation, and interpretation of armor and the arms they protected against.

The founder, John Woodman Higgins, may not have been Superman, but he was indubitably a "man of steel" who translated a childhood fascination with metallurgy into the co-founding of the Worcester Pressed Steel Company. The fascination with metals dovetailed with his boyhood attachment to chivalric tales and triggered the collecting impulse. Higgins became nearly obsessed with suits of armor and began purchasing them in 1914 when he was on his honeymoon. (No word on what his bride thought.) Within 15 years the private collection of suits of armor, chain mail, swords, shields, lances, and other examples of the armorer's art had outgrown his home.

So Higgins did what any steel magnate might have done: He built a museum for his prized collection and installed the headquarters of his company in the same building. Something of a minor art deco masterpiece, the building used a steel curtain wall introduced a few years earlier by Walter Gropius in his design of the Bauhaus Dessau.

Higgins Armory Museum:

With more than 100 suits of armor, this Worcester institution is dedicated to collecting, preserving, and exhibiting arms and armor.

Inside the museum, the Great Hall seems filled with the spirits of warriors past who once creaked and squeaked around in the great iron and steel suits of armor. Gleaming exhibits dissect the evolution of armor over 15 centuries, beginning with Roman armor of the 3rd century. Even the most devoted "Dungeons and Dragons" fan will be awed by more than 3,000 suits of armor or components from Europe, as well as more than 1,000 pieces of African, Islamic, Indian, and Japanese body defenses and arms.

Just pity the poor wretches who have to polish all those shiny surfaces!

You cross only a street, not a moat, to reach the Higgins Armory Museum at 100 Barber Avenue, Worcester. For more information, call (508) 853–6015 or visit www.higgins.org.

Kansas City, here you come. Check in with the hostesses at the Hilltop Steak House on Route 1 South in Saugus, and that's likely to be your destination. Or Sioux City. Or Dodge City. Those famous cattle towns are the names of the gymnasium-size dining rooms of the house of broiled beef that serves three million meals a year.

It's not like you weren't warned. The herd of life-size fiberglass cattle and the 30-foot-high green cactus are a giveaway that the Hilltop is no mom-and-pop restaurant. It's steak on steroids (not necessarily in the meat, but in the concept).

Actually, it *was* a mom-and-pop steak house. Frank Giuffrida bought the property in Saugus in 1961 and converted it to a western steak house. His wife, Irene, served as hostess. The creative landscaping was a way to catch drivers' attention as they whizzed by. The cattle are anchored in cement, just to keep them from wandering. (One steer found its way to the top of the school dome at the Massachusetts Institute of Technology in one of the famous student "hacks," or pranks, for which those budding geniuses are known.)

The Giuffridas sold the business in 1994, but the Hilltop continues to rope and roll and brand 'em. It even has a butcher shop if you like your porterhouse *really* rare. You can't make reservations, but you can get

Hilltop Steak House:

The landmark cattle and cactus outside Hilltop are just some of the roadside oddities on Route 1 in Saugus.

more information by calling (781) 233–7700 or visiting www.hilltopsteakhouse.com.

The Hilltop is not alone in its flights of architectural fancy on Route 1 just north of Boston. Prince Pizzeria & Bar (781–233–9950) entices diners with its landmark replica of Pisa's famed leaning tower (emblazoned "Tower of Pizza" in red neon). Ruggieri's at the Ship (781–595–7400), an Italian restaurant just north across the line in Lynnfield, occupies a 90-foot model brigantine, complete with bowsprit and busty figurehead, that seems to have run aground into a shopping center. South of the Hilltop, a 50-foot orange *T. Rex* marks a minigolf course.

you know you're in
massachusetts when...
...the old Chiefs still roar

The roar of straight pipes, the flash of chrome, the smell of hot rubber and gasoline fumes—the motorcycle is an iconic piece of the American experience. And while the Harley hogs may rule the roads today, it wasn't always thus. The first commercially manufactured gasoline-powered motorcycles in the world came out of the shop of the Hendee Manufacturing Company in Springfield in 1901.

Bicycle racer George M. Hendee and engineering whiz and Swedish immigrant Oscar Hedstrom had a brainstorm: They would marry Hendee's super-strong bicycles to Hedstrom's reliable little gasoline engine to create "a motor-driven bicycle for the everyday use by the general public." When the partners unveiled their creation—a chain-driven cycle that could reach the terrifying speed of 25 miles per hour—they decided to call the firm the Indian Motorcycle Company, in order to indicate a "wholly American product in the pioneering tradition."

In 1907 the New York Police Department purchased a pair of the new Twins. The officers praised the left-hand throttle that let them give chase and draw their sidearms at the same time. By 1919 the company was giving its models Indian-sounding names, starting with the Scout, soon followed by the Chief and then the Big Chief, a 1200cc monster. When the company dropped the *r* to become the Indian Motocycle Company

in 1923, doom was already on the horizon. At $285, the Model T Ford cost about the same as a Chief.

During World War II Indian produced its vehicles strictly for the military, but the firm cut a bad deal with the government and ended up cash-strapped. By 1953 sales had dwindled; the factory closed forever that August.

But thousands of old Indians are still on the road, treasured by collectors. The marque returned in 1999, but purists insist that the new "Indians" are pale imitations of the old bikes. Fortunately for aficionados, every Indian model manufactured through 1953 can be seen in running condition at the Springfield Indian Motocycle Museum, located at 33 Hendee Street. Call (413) 737–2624 for information.

Indian Motorcycle:

Springfield's Indian Motocycle Museum recalls the heyday of America's first mass-produced two-wheel cruisers in the brand's former factory complex.

you know you're in
massachusetts when...
...Irish eyes are smiling

There's an Irish pub in practically every Greater Boston neighborhood, and The Field in Cambridge alone serves more kegs of Guinness draught than any other establishment in the country. After the umpteenth pint of Guinness, fourth serving of shepherd's pie, and yet another rendition of "The Wind That Shakes the Barley," it's not surprising that visitors sometimes get a wee bit green about the gills. But there's a lot more Irish to the city than its public houses.

For one thing, there's the inescapably mournful side of Irish identity. Most Boston Irish Americans are descendants of famine refugees, and it's notable that there are two substantial memorials to the famine that killed one million and drove another two million to emigrate. The statue on the Cambridge Common shows a woman cradling her dead child and exhorting her teenage son to take a surviving child away to the New World. Boston's Irish Famine Memorial on Washington Street depicts *two* families, one wracked by the Great Hunger and the other beaming as they arrive in America.

Some 26 percent of Bostonians list their ancestry as Irish, and South Boston has been known at times as "Little Galway." Although there are larger numbers of Irish Americans in parts of New York City, overall, Boston is the greenest of American urban centers. The city welcomes 60,000 visitors a year from Ireland.

Things have certainly changed since the Great Hunger days, when immigrant job-seekers were met with signs informing them that "No Irish Need Apply." From the late 19th century, Irish Americans came to dominate city politics and moved into the boardrooms and bank offices. Thousands left the city to form posh enclaves on the South Shore, sometimes called the Irish-American Riviera.

The Boston Irish Heritage Trail, a 3-mile walking tour in the city with references to outlying South Shore sites, marks some of these achievements. For more information, visit www.irishheritagetrail.com.

Irish:

With roughly a quarter of residents in the Boston metropolitan area claiming Irish ancestry, the Hub is famously North America's most Irish city.

you know you're in
massachusetts when...
...dancers hit the Pillow

Eighteenth-century settlers indulged in a flight of fancy when they imagined that the zigzag road that climbed to a mountaintop farm in Becket resembled Jacob's Ladder. The farm family played along, calling their homestead Jacob's Pillow after the big boulder where Jacob could rest his head and dream of heaven.

The whimsical name stuck. Today, if Jacob were a dancer, he might indeed think that he had ascended to heaven. Such is the esteem that the Jacob's Pillow Dance Festival inspires.

If not heaven, the hilltop complex in this southern Berkshire town is, at the least, a National Historic Landmark, recognized for its role in nurturing contemporary dance. Enthusiastic audiences are the proof of the pudding.

In 1930 modern dance pioneer Ted Shawn made the farm his artistic haven and soon nurtured a company of male modern dancers. Beginning in 1942, he directed a yearly festival aimed at bringing the best of the dance world to the Berkshires. The Ted Shawn Theater, which opened that year and remains in operation, was the first theater in the country built specifically for dance performances. Its rustic exterior was designed to harmonize with the farm buildings and blend into the woodsy landscape. The rooftop weather vane—in the form of a muscular dancer with outstretched arms

Jacob's Pillow:

The Jacob's Pillow Dance Festival was founded in Becket in the 1940s, and its site was declared a National Historic Landmark in 2003.

and one leg thrust into the air—does, however, suggest that this isn't just another milking barn.

For three incredible summer months, modern dance masters, classical ballerinas, flamenco stars, and performers from all over the world make their way up the Ladder to the heights of the Pillow. As the festival has grown, it hasn't lost sight of the magical qualities of its hilltop setting. Dancers and audiences alike love the outdoor stage set in a grove of evergreens. Visitors are free to wander the grounds and grab a bite to eat until a bell rings to summon them to their seats.

It's fun to drive the twisting road to the Pillow, which is at 358 George Carter Road in Becket. For more information, call (413) 243–0749 or visit www.jacobspillow.org.

you know you're in
massachusetts when...
... baseball goes to bat for kids

All the drivers with the nifty Red Sox logo license plates on their cars aren't just proclaiming their love for their favorite sports team. They're also supporting the Jimmy Fund, the official charity of the Sox.

It began modestly enough in 1948, when a few members of the Hub's National League team of the time, the Boston Braves, took part in a national radio broadcast with a young cancer patient. Contributions poured in from listeners to help buy a television so that the patient (called "Jimmy" to protect his privacy) could keep up with the baseball season. Thus, the Jimmy Fund was born. When the Braves moved to Milwaukee in 1953, Boston Red Sox owners Tom and Jean Yawkey adopted the fund and began a commitment to a single charity that remains unrivaled in professional sports.

Over the years, the Jimmy Fund has helped to support treatments for patients—both children and adults—at the Dana-Farber Cancer Institute as well as research to find new methods of detection, treatment, and, eventually, a cure. Countless children have had their days brightened by a visit from their favorite player: Ted Williams, Carl Yastrzemski, Johnny Damon, and Tim Wakefield among many, many others. The original "Jimmy," Einar Gustafson, revealed his identity in 1998 and remained active in the fund until his death in 2001 at age 65.

Jimmy Fund:

Launched in 1948, the official charity of the Boston Red Sox benefits children and adults with cancer.

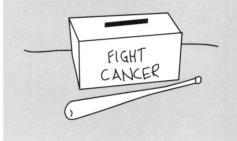

Sports enthusiasts of all types can help contribute to the cause through a variety of fund-raising events—from marathons to ski races, bike rides to sailing regattas, fishing tournaments to Boston Harbor swims. Visit www.jimmyfund.org for a full list of events. Hard-core baseball aficionados can channel their favorite Sox players at the annual John Hancock Fantasy Day at Fenway Park, when fans take to the field or try to hit a few pitches from a pitching machine. Knock one over the wall, and the Hancock kicks in an extra $2,000.

Pasadena has the Rose Bowl, the White House has the Rose Garden—but Boston has an entire park named Rose. So beloved was Rose Fitzgerald Kennedy (1890–1995) that once the interstate highway through Boston was buried underground, the people of Massachusetts named the park above it the Rose Kennedy Greenway after the matriarch of the state's political dynasty.

Rose Kennedy never held public office, but she must have had politics in her genes. Her father, John "Honey Fitz" Fitzgerald (1863–1950), served three terms as a U.S. congressman and was twice elected mayor of Boston. Her husband, Joseph Kennedy (1888–1969), was ambassador to Great Britain in the years leading up to World War II. Son John Fitzgerald Kennedy (1917–1963) served in the House and Senate and was the first Irish Catholic elected president. Son Robert Francis Kennedy (1925–1968) served as U.S. attorney general and a senator and was vying for his party's nomination for president when he was assassinated. Son Edward Moore Kennedy (b. 1932) was elected to the U.S. Senate in 1962 and became the conscience of the liberal wing of the Democratic Party. He hasn't left the post since.

The cult of personality looms large at Massachusetts polls. Voting for the Kennedys has always been accompanied by the sport of *watching* the Kennedys, including those not in public office. When the huge family gathers at the Hyannisport compound, reporters and paparazzi are never far away. Rarely does a Massachusetts newspaper print without some mention of a member of the clan in the political pages, society pages, or gossip columns.

The rise of the family fortune, from the modest home in Brookline where JFK was born to the pomp and circumstance of the Kennedy White House, parallels the ascendancy of the Boston Irish. The John F. Kennedy birthplace is at 83 Beals Street, Brookline. For information, call (617) 566–7937 or visit www.nps.gov/jofi. The John F. Kennedy Library and Museum is on Columbia Point in Boston. For information, call (617) 514–1600 or visit www.jfklibrary.org.

Kennedy Family:

This Massachusetts political dynasty stands in for royalty in our democracy.

VOTE KENNEDY

you know you're in
massachusetts when...
... magic never gets old

Le Grand David is not about to pull a disappearing act.

Anything but. "Marco the Magi's Production of Le Grand David and His Own Spectacular Magic Company" holds the Guinness World Record for longest-running stage magic show. That's a lot of rabbits. And a lot of hats. The production set the record in 1999, and no one has caught up to it yet.

The show premiered on February 20, 1977, at the Cabot Street Cinema Theatre, a restored 1920s performance hall in downtown Beverly. It's the brainchild of Cesareo Pelaez, who was entranced by traveling magic shows as a young boy growing up in Cuba. Pelaez founded his first magic troupe when he was a teenager. But rather than running away to join the circus, he went to college and eventually became a professor of psychology at Salem State College, practically next door to Beverly.

The magic show proved to be a wonderful diversion from Pelaez's academic life (he retired from Salem State in 1995). Though Pelaez may have a soft spot for the old-fashioned itinerant troupes of his youth, his own band of illusionists has stayed put, delighting generations of children from Massachusetts and beyond with the pratfalls of clowns and skills of jugglers. Adults puzzle over the illusions and sleights of

Le Grand David:

Holder of a Guinness World Record for longest-running magic show, the three-generation magic company has performed in Beverly since 1977.

hand. All in all, the 30-member troupe features three generations of magicians, countless costumes, and lavish sets.

Call (978) 927–3677 or visit www.legrand david.com for a show schedule. The Cabot Street Cinema Theatre is at 28 Cabot Street in Beverly. Even though the facility has 700 seats, it's smart to reserve in advance for these immensely popular performances.

Travelers entering Boston from the north pass through the city's newest ceremonial gateway: the wishbones and cables of the Leonard P. Zakim Bunker Hill Bridge. While most of the Big Dig—a decade-and-a-half, $14.6 billion construction project—buried interstate highways beneath Boston, the span vaulted through the air to cross the Charles River.

The bridge is the loveliest artifact of the largest and most complicated highway project ever undertaken in the core of a major American city. It is also a monument to the community activists and local politicians who balked at the twisted maze of interchanges originally planned as the river crossing.

Swiss bridge designer Christian Menn conceived a 1,457-foot cable-stayed suspension bridge as an elegant solution. Its 183-foot width accommodates 10 lanes of traffic, making it the widest bridge of its type when it was dedicated in 2002. The cable-stayed design eliminated the need to place support columns in the Charles River, leaving the waterway unimpeded for boaters and minimizing the impact on marine life. The 215 miles of white steel cables intentionally invoke the sails of a clipper ship, a reminder of Boston's maritime history.

Built for $105 million, the span rises to 322 feet on the north tower and 295 feet on the south tower. It was designed to withstand tornado-force winds of 400 miles per hour and an earthquake of 7.9 on the Richter scale, neither of which has ever been recorded in Boston.

The bridge's cumbersome name also echoes Boston's history of activism and aspiration. The peaks of the cable towers mimic the top of the nearby Bunker Hill Monument at the site of the Revolutionary War battle in Charlestown. But the name also honors a more recent hero, the late Leonard P. Zakim. Head of the New England chapter of the Anti-Defamation League for more than 20 years, Zakim was a leader in the struggle for civil rights in Boston and a builder of bridges across cultures and communities.

Leonard P. Zakim Bunker Hill Bridge:

At the time of its construction, this graceful span across the Charles River was the widest cable-stayed bridge in the world.

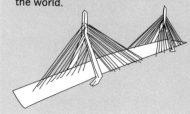

Spring announces itself in full splendor at the Arnold Arboretum, a former private estate in the Boston suburb of Jamaica Plain. Daffodils, early cherries, and magnolias jump-start the season in April. Crabapples, flowering quinces, and pears follow in early May. Next are the torch azaleas, dogwoods, horse chestnuts, and silver bells. But they're just a warm-up, so to speak, for the lilacs. By mid-May, almost 400 lilac plants along Bussey Hill begin to burst into bloom in a profusion of lavender hues, sending their sweet scent wafting on the gentle breezes.

The Arboretum's collection of more than 182 lilac types is one of the oldest in the country. To the delight of those who love spectacle, it's also one of the largest. Although lilacs are not native to the United States—most hail from Asia—they were already growing on the grounds when the Arnold Arboretum was founded in 1872. The ambitious plan called for nothing less than to bring together all the native and exotic trees and shrubs that can survive in New England weather. After more than a decade of hunting and gathering, planting began in 1885 and the Arboretum took shape following a landscape design by Frederick Law Olmsted.

Today, more than 7,000 plants grow on the 265-acre property. But it's no exaggeration to say that the lilac is first among its peers.

It's the only plant that has its own yearly party, complete with Morris dancers. Painters and photographers, families and couples turn out on Lilac Sunday to bask in the bloom and congratulate themselves for surviving another winter.

Call the Arboretum at (617) 524–1718 or visit www.arboretum.harvard.edu to get the date for Lilac Sunday. If you prefer to visit without the crowds, don't worry. The lilac bloom stretches on for five glorious weeks. But only on Lilac Sunday does the Arboretum bend the rules and allow picnics.

The Hunnewell Visitor Center is at the gate to the Arboretum, located at 125 Arborway. Stop to pick up a map.

Lilac Sunday:

The intense perfume of frilly blossom clusters draws thousands to Boston's Arnold Arboretum on the Sunday closest to May 20.

He stands there at the harbor in Gloucester, eyes fixed on the horizon and hands clutched on the wheel that guides his ship. His wet-weather gear lets you know there's a storm in progress. Beneath eight decades of verdigris, his jaw is clenched in determination.

The Man at the Wheel is the icon of Cape Ann, that bulge of granite that juts into the Atlantic 30 miles north of Boston. For nearly 400 years its villagers have looked to the sea, but the sea has not always looked back so kindly. At the statue's base and cemented into the sea wall that shields it from the waves, plaques with raised letters recite more than 10,000 names of Gloucester fishermen lost at sea since the first casualties in 1623.

Many Gloucester families have their tales of loss, and hardly a day goes by when some relative doesn't come down to the fishermen's memorial to lay a bouquet of flowers, run fingers over a loved one's name, and perhaps say a prayer. The names are in rough chronological order by death date, and the clusters tell terrible stories. In 1879 storms and accidents took 265 fishermen. Four years later the fleet was decimated again, with 249 lost. Eighteen of them were MacDonalds, likely every grown man in the family.

The Man at the Wheel:

This iconic statue in Gloucester harbor is surrounded by plaques listing the names of Gloucester fishermen lost at sea since 1623.

The closure of the Grand Banks to ground-fishing in recent decades has trimmed the number of voyages and the number of deaths, but fishermen still perish. The 1991 entry lists six men aboard the *Andrea Gale,* the swordfish boat featured in the book and movie *The Perfect Storm.* Don't look for George Clooney; he's still in Hollywood. But it's easy enough to find the name of the man he portrayed, Frank Billy Tyne Jr.

Less than 100 yards away stands the Fishermen's Wives and Families memorial. Dedicated in 2001, this memorial expresses the lot of Gloucester families, often suspended between fear and hope. A little boy clings to his mother's skirt, looking out to sea as if to say, "Is that my father's boat?"

Visitors to the Mapparium in Boston can't exactly sit on top of the world, but they can take a journey to the center of the earth via a glass walkway that cuts straight across it around the Tropic of Capricorn. It's a chance to really get into geography.

The Mapparium, a stained-glass globe 30 feet in diameter, was constructed between 1932 and 1935 at a cost of $8,900. After a $1 million renovation, it became the center-piece of the Mary Baker Eddy Library for the Betterment of Humanity at the Christian Science Headquarters.

The great globe is a masterpiece of both mapmaking and the craft of stained glass. Each of the 608 panels represents 10 degrees of latitude and longitude. The rich colors that define the individual countries and delineate land from water were derived from a mixture of pigments akin to those used in the 14th century. The colors were sprayed onto pieces of glass that were then baked and finally assembled within a bronze framework that also depicts the lines of longitude and latitude.

Because the "map" is a globe, it displays masses of land and water without the dis-torted proportions of two-dimensional rep-resentations. As the world continued to turn, the Mapparium's borders remained fixed in the 1930s. A sound-and-light show—206 LCD panels that produce 16 million colors—brings things up to date.

Mapparium:

Constructed between 1932 and 1935, this three-story glass globe has a pedestrian bridge through the core of the planet.

The presentation notes, for example, that today 75 percent of the world is demo-cratic, compared to only 20 percent when the Mapparium opened. At that time, Africa was dominated by a handful of colonial powers. Today the continent is divided into more than 50 independent countries. The former Soviet Union has split into inde-pendent nations.

A word of caution: If you don't want every-one in the world to know your thoughts, speak softly. Sound bounces off glass, so a whisper in America is audible in China.

The Mary Baker Eddy Library is at 200 Massachusetts Avenue. For more informa-tion, call (617) 450–7000 or visit www .marybakereddylibrary.org.

massachusetts when...

...art is the biggest thing around

Artists think big, and big ideas shouldn't be limited by physical space. That's the operating principle at the Massachusetts Museum of Contemporary Art (better known as Mass MoCA), which opened in 1999 in the former mill town of North Adams.

Throughout New England, abandoned mill buildings have found new life as loft condominiums and high-tech offices, but no transformation has had quite the élan of the Mass MoCA campus. The complex of 26 redbrick buildings was constructed between 1872 and 1900 for a textile manufacturer and was later converted to the production of electrical components. When the electrical company pulled out in 1985, a group of political and arts leaders thought big themselves—and hatched the radical idea that a contemporary arts center could breathe new life into a town seemingly destined for economic collapse.

Fourteen years and $31.4 million later, Mass MoCA opened as the largest contemporary visual arts and performing center in the country. Nineteen galleries boast more than 100,000 square feet of exhibition space. The Black Box and Lab Theaters are 10,000 square feet and 3,500 square feet, respectively. The screen for the outdoor cinema is 50 feet wide. One of the two performance courtyards occupies 22,500 square feet. In total, 300,000 square feet of the complex have been developed, leaving another 300,000 square feet in reserve.

So, what might a visitor expect besides giant canvases and oversize sculptures originally intended for outdoor spaces? Don't be surprised if you encounter a combination video-and-live-performance piece acting out an exhibit of paintings. In the past Mass MoCA has devoted an entire gallery to an environment cast in bronze—and an entire cavernous building to a temporary exhibition of a twisted series of amusement park rides designed to challenge psychological and physiological perception. Big thinkers need big spaces.

The Massachusetts Museum of Contemporary Art is located at 1040 Mass MoCA Way in North Adams. For more information, call (413) 662–2111 or visit www.massmoca .org.

Massachusetts Museum of Contemporary Art:

Opened in 1999 in a complex of late-19th-century mill buildings, Mass MoCA displays work too large in scale for conventional museum galleries.

you know you're in
massachusetts when...
...bureaucracy has a long tradition

Long before the federal government had even considered promulgating something as complex as the Internal Revenue Service or Homeland Security, Massachusetts was busy making up rules and regulations for everyone to live by. Consider the lot of the Pilgrims aboard the *Mayflower.* Through some devious maneuvers at court, they had obtained a charter from King James (whom they addressed as "our dread Sovereign Lord") to plant a colony in the northern reaches of Virginia. But after an arduous voyage (compounded by a shortage of beer), the first land they sighted was Cape Cod.

It was November, and winter was coming. The Pilgrims were anchored off what is now Provincetown, hundreds of miles off course and well outside the purview of their charter. People were sick and hungry (and desirous of beer). So the same wise planners who had waited until early September to set sail for America decided that, until everyone had agreed to certain rules and regulations, nobody could get off the boat to see if this was a worthwhile place to settle.

The document they drew up (which 41 of the 102 passengers signed) has come down to us as the Mayflower Compact. It marks the official beginning of bureaucracy in Massachusetts and establishes the law of rules as much as it imposes the rule of law.

In effect, the passengers agreed to consider themselves a single political body and to follow whatever "just and equal Laws, Ordinances, Acts, Constitutions and Offices, from time to time, as shall be thought most meet and convenient for the General good of the Colony."

It was the blank check of all blank checks, as they each promised "all due submission and obedience." A good modern lawyer probably could have found a loophole or two by arguing that at least some of the signatories jotted down their John Hancocks under duress. It was, after all, the only way off the ship.

And didn't a shortage of beer constitute cruel and unusual punishment?

Mayflower Compact:

The Pilgrims set up a government with laws, rules, and regulations before anyone could leave the ship to settle Massachusetts.

Call me Ishmael . . . So begins Herman Melville's account of the nearly impossible quest to find God in the face of an uncaring universe—or the author's riveting adventure story about whaling. Take your pick. The book in question, *Moby-Dick, or The Whale,* was based on Melville's own experiences aboard the *Acushnet,* a whaler that shipped out from New Bedford harbor on January 3, 1841.

Each year the New Bedford Whaling Museum marks the anniversary of Melville's departure with the Moby-Dick Marathon, where volunteers read the entire tome in about 25 hours.

In the museum, readers stand in front of the *Lagoda,* a half-size replica of a whaling bark, or in front of a mural of Moby-Dick. Father Mapple's sermon is read in the Seamen's Bethel; located across the street from the museum, this is one of the sites mentioned in Melville's classic. The museum and chapel are part of the 13-block New Bedford Whaling National Historical Park, which preserves much of the city's golden age (roughly 1830–1860) as the world's leading whaling port.

Nineteenth-century whalers plied the seven seas in pursuit of their quarry, braving the ice floes of the Arctic and Antarctic, the dead air of the horse latitudes, and the furious typhoons of the Pacific. With as little as an $84 advance (that's what Melville

Moby-Dick:

The annual nonstop reading of this literary classic marks the date that author Herman Melville shipped out of New Bedford aboard a whaling ship.

received), men would ship out for two or three years of dirty, dangerous work that made New Bedford shipowners rich.

As suddenly as the whaling boom began, it ended with the discovery of petroleum as an alternative to whale oil. By the end of the 19th century, New Bedford's whaling industry—and its prosperity—were gone.

Melville's tale has proved more enduring.

The New Bedford Whaling Museum is located at 18 Johnnycake Hill. For more information, call (508) 997–0046 or visit www.whalingmuseum.org. The visitor center for the New Bedford Whaling National Historical Park is located at 33 William Street. For more information, call (508) 996–4095 or visit www.nps.gov/nebe.

massachusetts when...

...the trail makes a hairpin turn

For the full sensory impact, drive the Mohawk Trail from east to west, beginning at the 782-foot French King Bridge that crosses a deep gorge of the Connecticut River between Erving and Gill. Distant mountain vistas make Massachusetts's most famous scenic byway a favorite with fall leaf peepers. But truth be told, it's just plain fun to drive the 63-mile route as it twists and turns and climbs over the Berkshire hills between the Connecticut and Housatonic valleys.

This centuries-old Native American footpath was widened to accommodate first horses and then wagons. After a $300,000 construction project, it opened for automobiles in 1914 and was immediately proclaimed the "most beautiful road in New England." Driving it today still taps into the sense of adventure of early motorists who labored up the hills in their Model Ts. Old-fashioned tourist attractions add retro charm to the vistas.

The Trail ascends steeply from Greenfield. Halfway up the first hill, the Long View Tower stands as an avatar of early auto touring, advertising views to distant Vermont and New Hampshire that are now partly obscured. About 15 miles west, Gould's Sugar House (413–625–6170) serves pancakes, waffles, and corn fritters during the spring maple syrup season and then reopens to feed the foliage crowds in the fall.

Mohawk Trail:

Follow the 63-mile route from east to west to get the full rush of the Hairpin Turn, a dramatic switchback as the trail descends into the Hoosic River valley.

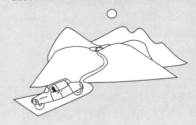

But the Trail's most famous landmark is the Big Indian Shop (413–625–6817), with its old-fashioned merchandise and eponymous statue out front. From here the Trail begins to snake through the Cold River gorge as it climbs steeply toward not one but two summits. Eastern Summit looks out 65 miles to the Green Mountains. But the view is even better 2 miles west at the Trail's highest point, the 2,110-foot Whitcomb Summit. Peaks of Massachusetts, New Hampshire, and Vermont all bristle on the horizon.

The best is yet to come: After a series of switchbacks on the western slopes, the Mohawk Trail hits the aptly named Hairpin Turn—the Trail's most dramatic switchback—before it whooshes down to the river valley floor a thousand feet below.

you know you're in
massachusetts when...
... visions of a red fish shack keep cropping up

It's almost impossible not to snap a photo of the little red building perched on a granite-block wharf in Rockport Harbor—unless you prefer to set up your easel and pull out your paintbrushes. The building has been painted and photographed so often that it was a natural to grace the Massachusetts stamp in the "Greetings from America" series introduced by the U.S. Postal Service in 2002.

The landmark began as a humble fishing gear shack on Bradley Wharf on Rockport's Bearskin Neck. In the 1870s, artists drawn to the gorgeous light at the tip of Cape Ann began flocking to the village, and they found the technical challenge of capturing the fish shack's blocky cubes and the light shimmering on the water irresistible. Illustrator and etcher Lester Hornby (1882–1956), who taught in both Paris and Rockport, is said to have dubbed the scene "Motif No.1" because so many of his students chose it as their subject.

Artists appropriated more than just the image of the fish shack. They soon converted many of the fish shacks along Bearskin Neck into combined studio and gallery spaces. Motif No.1 itself served as the studio of artist John Buckley (1891–1958) in the 1930s. (He sold it to the town in 1945.) The Rockport Art Association (12 Main Street; 978–546–6604) was founded in 1921. To this day, artists and fishers coexist on the Neck, finding common ground, so to speak, in their love of the sea.

Disaster struck when the Blizzard of 1978 felled Motif No.1. A replica in the conventional board-and-batten building style rose from the rubble in less than a year and was dedicated on November 26, 1978. Its weathered appearance came from a specially formulated wood stain that replicated the mixture of crankcase oil and red paint that had been applied to the original to reduce glare and maximize its rustic look.

In May, Rockport celebrates the coming of spring with Motif No.1 Days. For information, call the Rockport Chamber of Commerce at (978) 546–6575 or (888) 726–3922 or visit www.rockportusa.com.

Motif No. 1:

The dark red fish shack on Bearskin Neck in Rockport Harbor is a perennially favored subject for professional and amateur artists alike.

Talk about a fish out of water. A lighthouse originally designed for the Charles River was instead firmly planted at the opposite end of the state. The 93-foot granite tower marks the 3,491-foot summit of Massachusetts's tallest peak, Mount Greylock. Its beacon—visible for 70 miles—serves aviators rather than navigators.

Established in 1898, Mount Greylock was the commonwealth's first state park. The lighthouse design was given a new purpose as the Veterans War Memorial Tower in 1933, dedicated to all Massachusetts sons and daughters who lost their lives as casualties of war. Actually, the 1930s marked a time of great activity on the mountain as numerous projects enhanced its recreational potential and made it more accessible to the public. The Civilian Conservation Corps upgraded roads, created hiking trails, and completed the construction of Bascom Lodge, a welcoming rest spot for hikers at the summit, practically in the shadow of the War Memorial.

Today, the state park encompasses 11,000 acres that are crossed by 50 miles of hiking trails, including a stretch of the Appalachian Trail. Those who seek the summit can take the easy way—the auto road—or the more contemplative approach on foot along a hiking path. It's worth the trip for the 100-mile views of the Taconic, Hoosac, and Catskill mountain ranges.

From Memorial Day through Columbus Day, the War Memorial is open daily. Although it was not designed with an outside observation deck, the winding interior staircase offers views through narrow slits in the upper walls. The extra height doesn't really improve the view. The reward is in the bragging rights for those who want to say that they truly made it to the top.

Before embarking on a climb, it's a good idea to check in at the Mount Greylock State Reservation Visitor Center on Rockwell Road in Lanesborough. For information, call (413) 499–4262 or visit www.mass .gov/dcr/parks/western/mgry.htm.

Mount Greylock:

The Veterans War Memorial Tower and Bascom Lodge are but two of the attractions at Mount Greylock, the state's highest mountain.

With a globe- and history-straddling permanent collection, Boston's Museum of Fine Arts (MFA) is among the world's largest museums. Its holdings range from Roman portrait busts to African masks, Chinese tomb figures to Mayan ceramics, Russian bassoons to American quilts—not to mention Dutch still-life paintings and Italian triptychs. To accommodate more than 450,000 objects, the MFA has broken ground for a new wing.

The MFA moved to its current site in 1909 and last added a new wing in 1981 for temporary exhibitions, a museum shop, a cafe, and a restaurant. But for the grandest effect, go in the original Huntington Street entrance of the granite classical revival building and ascend the marble staircase to the central rotunda, where American artist John Singer Sargent painted murals of Greek mythological figures.

Before photography, portraiture was the singular art. John Singleton Copley painted many Revolutionary War–era Boston bigwigs, and the MFA has about 60 of his works, including portraits of John Hancock, Samuel Adams, and Paul Revere. The collections also include stunning examples of Revere's work as a silversmith.

The MFA and Harvard University joined forces for major archaeological digs in Egypt and Sudan in the early 20th century.

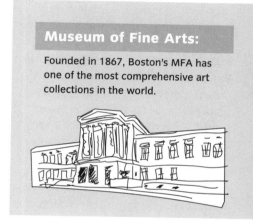

Museum of Fine Arts:

Founded in 1867, Boston's MFA has one of the most comprehensive art collections in the world.

As a result, the MFA has an enviable collection of Old Kingdom and Nubian art and artifacts displayed in serene galleries with low lighting. Mummies from three millennia are among the most popular objects in the museum.

The biggest crowds typically gather in the Impressionist galleries. Though Bostonians notoriously cling to the past, 19th-century collectors were smitten with the new French Impressionist paintings. Their generosity and other shrewd acquisitions made the MFA's holdings of works by Claude Monet among the world's largest. (His contemporaries are also well-represented.)

The Museum of Fine Arts is located at 465 Huntington Avenue. For more information, call (617) 267–9300 or visit www.mfa.org.

More than 100 ways to say "I love you" have been at the heart of the New England Confectionary Company since 1902. NECCO, as this survivor from the days when Boston and Cambridge dominated the national candy business is better known, produces more than eight billion Sweethearts® Conversation Hearts each Valentine's season, most of them in its Revere manufacturing plant.

Originally called Motto Hearts, the sweets are the direct conceptual descendants of late-19th-century hollow candies that were shaped like seashells and contained printed sayings on colored strips of paper. In 1866 the brother of NECCO's founder invented a technique to print directly onto the candy. The company didn't think to launch the tiny hearts, however, until 1902. They were an immediate success, and the entire production run sells out each year in about eight weeks.

Some original sentiments have stood the test of time, including "Be Mine," "Be Good," "Be True," "My Man," "Kiss Me," and "Sweet Talk." In the 1990s the company decided to get with the times by issuing hearts with such notations as "Email Me," "Fax Me," and "CU L8R." Each year, the company receives thousands of suggestions from romantics, school children, and candy lovers around the world. In 2006 NECCO introduced its first conjunction and

preposition (*and* and *to*) to enable hearts-lovers to spell out more complex messages using multiple candies, such as "Kiss Me" "To" "Be Mine."

NECCO officials say that the candy formulation and production technique has not changed since Conversation Hearts were introduced. They are made from the same batter as the company's signature NECCO Wafers. True to their name, Sweethearts® are 90 percent sugar, with dashes of corn syrup, gelatin, gums, and artificial colors and flavorings. The dough is rolled out and printed with sayings and cut into the heart shapes. The individual pieces are dried for 45 minutes to bring them to their tooth-chipping but mouthwatering consistency.

NECCO:

The New England Confectionery Company has been turning out Conversation Hearts for Valentine's Day since 1902.

massachusetts when...

...Patriots-ism is a way of life

The symbol may be more than two centuries old, but the enthusiasm is very 21st century. The New England Patriots came out of the huddle as one of the dominant professional football teams of the new millennium, with three quick championships in Super Bowls XXXVI, XXXVIII, and XXXIX. It was a surprisingly strong showing for an American conference team that had played in only two previous Super Bowls and had been steamrolled both times.

For the first decade of the franchise (founded in November 1959 as the Boston Patriots), the team played its home games on other people's turf: Boston University Field, Harvard Stadium, Fenway Park, and Boston College Alumni Stadium. Bay Staters took their time warming to the idea of professional football, this being a baseball domain. Football was simply that quaint, grunting sport played by college boys, most notably Harvard and Yale.

The Patriots began to hit their stride when they moved way out of town—to Foxboro, which is closer to Providence, Rhode Island, than to Boston—for the 1971 season and changed their name to embrace the entire region.

But in true Massachusetts fashion, the Patriots became a force in the National Football League through a combination of smarts (i.e., the strategies of coach Bill

New England Patriots:

Exiled from Boston to the netherworld of Foxboro, the region's professional football team is an autumnal religion for many Bay Staters.

Belichick) and the specialized skills of players like former kicker Adam Vinatieri, whose 48-yard kick won Super Bowl XXXVI as time ran out and gave the Patriots their first NFL championship. Two years later, Vinatieri reprised that kick with a 41-yard field goal with nine seconds on the clock to give the Pats (as they are affectionately known) a 32–29 Super Bowl win. In 2005 the hero was quarterback Tom Brady in a 24–21 win.

Everybody loves a winner, even in Red Sox country, and "Patriots Pride" is now the unofficial post-October sports religion of the Bay State. For ticket information, call the Gillette Stadium ticket line at (800) 543–1776 or visit www.patriots.com.

With cafe televisions tuned to European soccer matches, restaurants serving up bowls of pasta, and bakeries offering cannoli and biscotti, there's no question that the North End is Boston's own Little Italy.

Italian immigrants claimed the city's oldest neighborhood as their own more than a century ago and almost immediately began to stage religious festivals to honor the patron saints of the villages they had left behind. Despite creeping gentrification, more than 40 percent of North End residents still have Italian roots, and a dozen religious societies (of more than 50 originally) remain active today. That's enough to fill the narrow, old streets with pageantry practically every weekend from early June until late August—a concentration of Italian religious festivals rivaled only by those in Chicago and New York.

Green, white, and red *tre-colore* flags fly, and confetti rains down from apartment house windows. Marching bands keep time, and members of a religious society hoist their saint's statue on their shoulders for a winding procession through the neighborhood. Children and adults step out from the crowd to pin dollar bills to the image of Saint Anthony, Saint Rocco, Saint Joseph, Saint Lucy, or whatever saint is being honored that day. The funds help support charitable works, so it's a good idea for spectators to pitch in by buying a program or perhaps a small festival pin.

The festivals are also referred to as feasts, which is a particularly apt term. After a procession, the North End turns to what it does best: celebrating life, family, and friendship with heaping plates of food. Street vendors cook up sausage and onions, roast impaled pieces of lamb or chicken over charcoal, simmer corn on the cob in huge kettles, fill cannoli on the spot, slice pizzas, and scoop gelato. All the while there's music in the air, from the traditional Italian march tunes played by the likes of the Roma Band to Italian folksingers, Sinatra-style crooners, Neapolitan accordionists, doo-wop artists, and folk dancers on the temporary bandstand.

For information on the religious societies and their festival dates, visit www.northend boston.com.

North End Festivals:

Sausages sizzle and children rush to pin money on statues of patron saints as Boston's North End celebrates its Italian roots almost weekly throughout the summer.

Welcome to the 17th century—the year 1627, to be exact.

Just seven years after the plucky band of Pilgrims stepped ashore (whether on the fabled Rock or not), their little settlement of thatched-roofed cottages surrounded by a stockade stretched from the dual-duty fort and meetinghouse at the crest of a hill down to the edge of the ocean.

At Plimoth Plantation, a painstakingly accurate replica of the original, the calendar stopped at 1627. It's hard to tell who's more unsettled by the time warp: 21st-century visitors to the historic village or the colonists themselves, who are portrayed with all their petty foibles and grand aspirations by the Plantation's costumed staff.

Mention a hit TV show, the new hot prospect for the Red Sox, or the latest political scandal, and these colonial imposters will greet you with a blank stare or a derisive comment in Elizabethan English. Ditto for dishwashers, telephones, indoor plumbing, and all the other modern conveniences that prove unfathomable to the 17th-century pioneers.

Each interpreter channels an actual Plimoth resident, including William Bradford, the colony's second governor. His long-suffering wife Alles might even confide that she sometimes chafes at her husband's over-

Plimoth Plantation:

Re-enactors at this living history museum channel individual Plimoth settlers of 1627.

bearing nature. Gossiping, it seems, has a venerable history in our country. Our Pilgrim forefathers and -mothers liked to talk about their neighbors. Tongues must have wagged when Priscilla Mullins spurned military commander Myles Standish in favor of more modest cooper John Alden. Thanks to poet Henry Wadsworth Longfellow, their story survives to this day.

It's easy to relate to romantic intrigue but much harder to imagine how the Pilgrims had time for romance after long days of backbreaking labor. Creature comforts were scarce in their small, dark cottages, which had few windows, an open hearth, dirt floors, and almost no privacy.

But survive they did. Even today, one-tenth of the residents of the modern town of Plymouth claim to be descended from *Mayflower* passengers.

One wag dubbed them the "Friday night flights," referring to weekly gallery hopping in Provincetown between Memorial Day and Labor Day (aka The Season). A dozen or more galleries in this town at the tip of Cape Cod schedule openings for Friday night and ply the crowds with Chilean jug wine and assorted munchies. If you consider hard and soft cheeses to be separate food groups from mystery dip and raw vegetables, it's possible to pick up a balanced meal through judicious grazing. When the galleries close (come back on Saturday to buy), the movable feast moves on to cafes, bars, and artists' studios.

Provincetown (P'town to the locals) has been summer art central for more than a century. No one recorded whether Charles W. Hawthorne announced "Let there be light" when he climbed off the stagecoach in Provincetown in the 1890s, but by 1899 he was teaching *plein air* painting at the P'town waterfront in the summer to augment his winter classes at New York's Art Students League. Bohemians of one sort or another have been painting the town ever since.

Two institutions have had some success herding these cats. The Hawthorne crowd—artists and patrons with Impressionist sensibilities—founded the Provincetown Art Association (PAA) in 1914. Although the organization languished during the Depression and World War II (when

Provincetown:

P'town has been a flourishing art colony since the late 1890s.

Edward Hopper was living and painting just two towns away), it served as a center for the explosion of abstract expressionism in the late 1940s and 1950s. The newly expanded PAA museum, located at 460 Commercial Street, features changing exhibitions from its in-depth collection of works by more than 500 artists associated with the Outer Cape. For information, call (508) 487–4372 or visit www.paam.org.

Some of the PAA artists were instrumental in founding the other magnet institution in the arts scene, the Fine Arts Work Center (FAWC). The center hosts fellowship residencies for artists and writers across the winter, and the FAWC Gallery at 24 Pearl Street shows the works of fellows. For information, call (508) 487–9960 or visit www.fawc.org.

you know you're in
massachusetts when...
...a water project creates a wilderness

Folks who live in the immediate vicinity simply call it "the Quabbin," remaining deliberately vague about whether they're speaking of the reservoir, the watershed, or the state park. The Quabbin is all three—and something more. In the heart of one of the more densely populated states, the Quabbin is a 56,000-acre tract of near-wilderness around a 412-billion-gallon lake. It is the home of deer, coyotes, bears, and eagles, as well as a place where imagination roams freely enough that some visitors claim to have spotted a mountain lion as well.

These woods most lovely, dark, and deep weren't always untamed forest. Early in the 20th century, state engineers determined that eastern Massachusetts lakes, springs, and wells would be inadequate to slake the thirst of Greater Boston. Surveys and hydrologic studies showed, however, that damming the Swift River would create a reservoir of nearly limitless clean, fresh water.

When the plan was implemented in the 1930s, the four Swift River villages of Dana, Prescott, Enfield, and Greenwich were simply wiped off the map, their 2,500 residents dispersed to the winds. Hundreds of homes and businesses were moved or dismantled. More than 6,000 graves from 34 cemeteries were moved to Quabbin Park Cemetery, outside the perimeter of the reservoir lake.

The Quabbin exists primarily to provide drinking water for more than two million people, but the public can use the lake and surrounding forest for activities that don't threaten the water supply. Fishing and boating are tightly controlled, and hikers are asked to use specific entry gates. An attentive walker heading toward the water—a hike of up to a mile from certain gates—will observe signs of past lives in a half-filled cellar hole, a patch of daffodils where a front door once stood, or a stand of apple or cherry trees that marks a backyard orchard.

Exhibits at the Quabbin Park Visitor Center, located at 485 Ware Road (Route 9) in Belchertown, detail the creation of the Quabbin. For information, call (413) 323–7221 or visit www.mass.gov/dcr/parks/central/quabbin.htm.

Quabbin:

In addition to slaking the thirst of eastern Massachusetts, the "drowned valley" of the Quabbin Reservoir turned four towns into 187 square miles of wilderness.

...one town claims two presidents

It took 36 administrations and more than 175 years before the Adams family claim as the only father-son pair of U.S. presidents was broken. But the town of Quincy, once part of Braintree, still holds its title as the birthplace of both members of a presidential dynasty. (George H. W. and George W. Bush were born in Milton, Massachusetts, and New Haven, Connecticut, respectively). What's more, the Adams homes are the country's oldest existing presidential birthplaces.

John Adams (1735–1826), the country's second president, was born in a 1681 saltbox dwelling. His father—a farmer, shoemaker, church deacon, and town selectman—sent John to Harvard. When he married Abigail in 1764, the newlyweds moved to a 1663 saltbox on the family property, where John also conducted his law practice. Three years later, John Quincy Adams (1767–1848) was born. The family stayed put during the Revolutionary War, though the elder John was often absent, attending to the business of founding a new country.

Both homes are now part of the Adams National Historical Park, where rangers discuss the family's modest origins and trace their rising fortunes. From the birthplaces, a trolley shuttles visitors to Peacefield, the much more elaborate mansion that John and Abigail purchased in 1788 on their return to Massachusetts after John's service as the first U.S. ambassador to England. John Adams called his estate "but the farm of a patriot." The town of Quincy likes to refer to it as "the first summer White House," since John and J. Q. called it home during their respective administrations (each served one term). Either way, the house's Cantonese china, European furniture, Oriental carpets, and 14,000-book library are ample evidence of a family made good.

The homes are open to visitors from mid-April through mid-November. Trolley tours depart from the Adams National Historical Park Visitor Center in Presidents Place Galleria at 1250 Hancock Street. For a schedule and more information, call (617) 770–1175 or visit www.nps.gov/adam.

Quincy:

John Adams and his son John Quincy Adams, the country's second and sixth presidents, respectively, were born here.

you know you're in
massachusetts when...
...nuptials are for everyone

At 12:01 A.M. on May 17, 2004, Marcia Harris and Susan Shepherd received a marriage license in the City of Cambridge. Some 226 other couples followed suit across the day, and throughout the Bay State, city and town offices issued more than 1,000 marriage licenses for same-sex couples. Already boasting the lowest divorce rate in the United States (2.4 per 100 marriages), Massachusetts welcomed another segment of its population to the state of matrimony.

The historic event was the result of a Supreme Judicial Court ruling—on a 4–3 split decision—that it is unconstitutional to deny civil marriage to gay couples. It was hardly the first time that Massachusetts had found itself on a different side of a social issue from much of the country.

In 1783 the Supreme Judicial Court unanimously ruled that slavery was illegal, based on the justices' reading of article 1 of the state constitution, which begins "All men are created free and equal. . . ." The ruling prompted John Adams to write a new Massachusetts constitution—not to permit slavery but to codify its abolition. Massachusetts went on to play a leading role in the abolitionist movement in the years before the Civil War.

History hasn't upheld all of Massachusetts's attempts at reform. The Massachusetts Society for the Suppression of Intemperance (MSSI), first convened in 1813, was adamantly opposed to profanity and strongly in favor of observing the Sabbath. The MSSI position on alcohol—that drinking was fine in moderation—didn't quite resonate with the Prohibitionists elsewhere.

Other reformers fell short as well. Bay State suffragists convened the first national women's rights convention in Worcester in 1850, but two decades later they could not convince their home state to restore the women's voting rights stripped away in the 1780 Constitution.

Massachusetts social reformers don't always win the first time out of the box, but they always come out swinging.

Reformers:

Massachusetts has a long and proud history of social reform, including its status as the first state in the country to allow same-sex marriage.

The one roadway challenge known to throw fear into the heart of an otherwise fearless (and, some might say, heartless) Massachusetts driver is the cloverleaf exchange—a mass of asphalt virtually never seen in the Bay State.

When several roads converge in Massachusetts, drivers instead run a tortuous gauntlet known innocently as a *rotary*. The English, who as everyone knows drive on the wrong side of the road to begin with, call this form of road interchange a *roundabout*. In England these configurations are approached timidly. An Englishman who picks up a rental car after arriving at Logan International Airport usually responds to his first rotary by coming to a complete stop.

Until he's rear-ended.

The art of driving in a rotary bears a strong resemblance to skydiving or bungee jumping. You have to take the leap and believe that it will all work out. By law, any vehicle entering a rotary must yield to all other vehicles already in the rotary. In practice, this is accomplished by observing rotary traffic from a distance, gunning the engine, and matching your vehicle's speed to that of the vehicles in the rotary. This operation must be timed so that you enter the rotary precisely when a car-length gap is provided by some out-of-state driver who has failed to close ranks by tailgating.

Rotary:

The Bay State favors the free-for-all rotary as the easiest way to merge several streams of traffic.

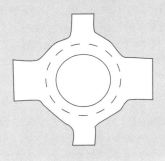

Multiple-lane rotaries are never marked with lane lines but can be identified by sight. If the road is wide enough for you to squeeze past another car, it's a two-lane rotary. Thus, the most efficient way to negotiate a rotary is to enter in the extreme outside lane and stay there until you peel off onto your chosen route. Unfortunately, everyone else also knows this. Using your directional signal will not help. Most Massachusetts drivers consider blinkers a fashion accessory.

Like government buildings everywhere, the Massachusetts State House in Boston is festooned with paintings, statues, and stained glass windows that memorialize and celebrate famous people, places, and events.

But probably the best-known public art object is an approximately 5-foot-long wooden carving of a fish. A codfish, to be exact. The carving was a gift from merchant John Rowe in 1784. It hung above the Hall of Representatives in what is now the Old State House "as a memorial to the importance of the Cod-Fishery to the welfare of the Commonwealth." The British royal symbols of the lion and the unicorn may have staked their claim on the building's facade, but the colonists knew where their priorities lay. So many of Boston's fine old families made their fortunes from the fishing industry that they continued to be known as the "codfish aristocracy" long after they moved on to railroads, oil wells, and banking.

In 1798, when the legislators moved into the new State House designed by Charles Bulfinch on the summit of Beacon Hill, they brought the Sacred Cod with them. It now hangs in the gallery above the House of Representatives. Because it is a symmetrical carving, it can be hung pointing in either direction. Some say it always faces the party in power.

The totemic qualities of this wooden fish have given it something akin to the status of a religious icon over the years. The Massachusetts House will not convene if the pine carving is absent. When the staff of the *Harvard Lampoon* (Harvard's humor magazine) snatched the forefathers' fish on April 26, 1933, the House leadership brought all legislative business to a screeching halt for several days. An oft-repeated version of the tale says that the pranksters eventually tipped off the furious legislators that they had stashed the Sacred Cod in a State House closet.

If you'd like to check out the Sacred Cod and the other public art in the State House, call (617) 727–3676 for a schedule of guided tours.

Sacred Cod:

This pine carving of a fish has overseen Massachusetts legislative debate since 1784.

you know you're in
massachusetts when...
...Revolutionary courage comes in a bottle

Boston beer-drinkers have had many loves among local suds, but few beers have shown the staying power of a cold bottle named for a hot-blooded leader of the Sons of Liberty. Until Jim Koch selected Samuel Adams as the namesake for the flagship lager of the Boston Beer Company, few knew that the Revolutionary provocateur had been a brewer himself.

Second cousin to the man who would become the second U.S. president (see page 76), Samuel Adams went into the brewing business with his father right after college (Harvard, of course). When the brewery went bust in 1764, Adams turned from fermenting barley to fomenting rebellion and spent the rest of his life in Massachusetts politics. He was a ringleader in the Boston Tea Party (who would expect a brewer to have sympathy for tea?) and one of the most vocal members of the Continental Congress to press for revolution. When he finally got the independent country he wanted, Sam Adams was leery of its central government, speaking for ratification of the Constitution only if the Bill of Rights was added to protect the people.

Jim Koch couldn't have selected a feistier figure to help him to become the first small-scale commercial brewer to successfully challenge the pale beers that had dominated America for a half century after the end of Prohibition. Working with an 1870s family recipe, Koch introduced his Samuel Adams Boston Lager to about two dozen bars and restaurants in April 1985. It was the beginning of the microbrew revolution to restore flavor to American beer, and Sam Adams was, once again, in the revolutionary vanguard.

Although this 800-pound gorilla of the microbrew movement farms out a lot of its production to contract brewers around the country, the company keeps a small facility at 30 Germania Street in Jamaica Plain, in the heart of what was the Germanic brewing district of Boston before Prohibition. The brewery is open for tours and tastings. For information on the company, call (617) 482–1332 or visit www.samadams.com. For information on tours, including directions, call (617) 368–5080.

Samuel Adams:

The Boston Beer Company named its flagship suds to conjure the feisty spirit of Boston patriot, brewer, and legendary imbiber Sam Adams.

Few fish are such chameleons as scrod, that staple of Boston restaurant menus and weight-loss cookbooks. Traditionally served roasted or broiled with buttered bread crumbs on top, Boston scrod is the ultimate in white food. Indeed, most restaurants cook it in a white ceramic au gratin pan and serve it on a white plate with a pale wedge of lemon and a springy sprig of parsley. People love it. Little old ladies on Beacon Hill practically survive on it. Millions of tourists who need a change from lobster gobble it up every year.

Too bad that there is actually no such thing as scrod. Along with its eponymous dinner rolls and Boston Cream Pie, the venerable Omni Parker House in Boston is refreshingly candid about the word *scrod*. The hotel not only proudly defines it as the "freshest catch of the day," but also takes credit for introducing the term.

Some *really* old-fashioned Bay State restaurants will give subtle hints about what's on your plate. They use the spelling "scrod" if it is young codfish (or the tail of a big codfish) but spell the entree "schrod" if the fish in question happens to be haddock, which most cod fishermen catch in the same waters at the same depth. Of course, should the dish be made with pollock (another member of the family), no one will spell it "scpod" as a tip-off.

Scrod:

Enshrined as a classic in regional restaurants, "scrod" is as likely to be haddock or pollock as codfish, depending on prices at the morning fish auction.

With the traditional preparation, all three fish taste pretty much the same, though cod has bigger flakes, a firmer texture, and—some diners say—better flavor.

Walking tours of Boston's Black Heritage Trail depart from the Shaw Memorial sculpture at the summit of Beacon Hill across from the State House. In the first decades of American independence, many of Boston's free African-American families lived on the slopes of Beacon Hill. In the years leading up to the Civil War, the city was a stop on the Underground Railroad and a hotbed of abolitionist activity.

The Shaw Memorial honors the 54th Massachusetts Volunteer Infantry, which went down in history as the first free black regiment from the northern states to fight in the Civil War. The regiment was led by Colonel Robert Gould Shaw, scion of one of Boston's fine old Brahmin families. Less than three months after the regiment was formed, the soldiers proved themselves in a heroic, but ultimately doomed, assault on Fort Wagner, near Charleston, South Carolina. Shaw and many of his men gave their lives in the battle.

The 1989 movie *Glory*, starring Morgan Freeman, Denzel Washington, and Matthew Broderick (the latter depicted Shaw), does a fine job telling the tale of the regiment's bravery and tenacity. But sculptor Augustus Saint-Gaudens's masterpiece has proven more enduring.

Beginning with the idea of an equestrian statue of Shaw (which the colonel's mother opposed as too "grandiose"), Saint-Gaudens labored for almost 14 years to create an innovative piece of artistry. The 11-by-14-foot work does feature Shaw on horseback, but he is anchored by images of his men in profile as they march with their rifles on their shoulders. Each figure stands out from the whole with dignity and a sense of purpose. So moving is Saint-Gaudens's work that many point to it as one of the finest sculptural memorials of the 19th century.

In an oversight not lost on Boston's African-American community, the names of soldiers who died at Fort Wagner were not added to the memorial until 1982.

For more information about the Black Heritage Trail and for a schedule of walking tours, call (617) 742–5415 or visit www.nps.gov/boaf.

Shaw Memorial:

This masterpiece sculpture by Augustus Saint-Gaudens honors the 54th Regiment, the first all-black force recruited in the North to fight for the Union in the Civil War.

you know you're in
massachusetts when...
... roses grow on rooftops

If you want to blend in on Nantucket, be sure to adopt the island's unisex wardrobe: deck shoes, shorts, and a pastel polo shirt. If the weather's cool, tie a sweater around your shoulders. And whatever you do, don't try to pronounce the full name of Siasconset. The little village at the eastern end of the island is simply known as 'Sconset.

'Sconset started life around 1700 as a look-out post for whales. During the early days of Nantucket's whaling industry, hunters concentrated on the leviathans that swam too close to shore. Over time, 'Sconset evolved into one of Nantucket's major fishing villages. Many of the quaint—and highly coveted—cottages were built by fishermen more than a century and a half ago, often from salvaged materials that had washed ashore.

Well-heeled vacationers discovered 'Sconset in the late 19th century, and it soon became the darling of the Manhattan theater crowd. (A 'Sconset address still carries a lot of cachet.) The village boasts a post office, a grocery store, and a couple of restaurants. It's the ultimate in simple chic.

That's another thing you need to know about the island. Old-line Nantucketers decry conspicuous consumption and the proliferation of McMansions. They prefer to cloak their wealth in a modest exterior — which means cedar shingles weathered to

Siasconset:

Former fishermen's cottages in this Nantucket Island village are covered with lattices for growing roses on rooftops.

a pearly gray. White picket fences are allowed. So are window boxes. One of the few excesses in this sedate little enclave are the trellises that often run up the side of a cottage and across the slanted roof to encourage roses to climb. By midsummer the rose-covered cottages of 'Sconset look like something out of a fairy tale.

The most enjoyable way to reach 'Sconset is via the nearly flat 10-mile Polpis Bike Path, which originates in the island's main town, also called Nantucket. The path skirts cranberry bogs and passes the red-and-white-striped Sankaty Head Lighthouse, which has warned ships off Nantucket's shoals since 1861. Bike rental shops cluster near the ferry docks. Be forewarned: Nantucketers frown on motor scooters.

We've all heard of whispering pines, babbling brooks, and sighing breezes, but who ever heard of a singing beach? Few strands make a sound as sweet as the real Singing Beach at Manchester-by-the-Sea, sandwiched between Boston's North Shore and the south side of the rocky Cape Ann peninsula.

That peculiar location is the key to why the sands sing. While most beach sand is a mixture of rock particles, clay, and smashed shell (and a certain amount of flotsam), the sand at Singing Beach consists of nearly pure quartz crystals. Cape Ann's granite jaw thrusts so far out to sea that it bears the brunt of ocean storms, protecting Manchester from strong currents and big waves. As rain, snow, and wind erode the winter beach, the sand washes into a pool a short distance below the low-tide line. Normally, currents and storm waves would wash the sand away, but at Singing Beach it just sits there, waiting to be brought back ashore in the spring.

Back and forth, back and forth the sand has moved for millennia, raked by the water until virtually identical grains of pure quartz are all that remain. When you drag your feet just right in the sands of Singing Beach, they "squeak." Draw out the stroke, and they might even ring with a bell-like tone, akin to the sound you get by rubbing the

Singing Beach:

Thanks to a peculiar conjunction of geological conditions, the sands of this Manchester beach make a singing sound when you walk on them.

wet rim of a glass. All the particles near the pressure of your foot are resonating. The phenomenon is so rare that you'd have to go all the way to Barking Sands on Kauai, Hawaii, to find a more outspoken shore.

you know you're in
massachusetts when...
...ice cream is mashed with candy

Back in the dark old days before cookies 'n' cream and Heath bar crunch ice creams came in pint containers from the grocery store, Steve Herrell had a vision.

The premium ice cream pioneer opened a modest little shop in Somerville in 1973. There he sold the exceptionally rich and creamy ice cream that he managed to turn out by modifying a commercial ice cream freezer. But decadent ice cream in unusual flavors wasn't enough. Herrell raised the standard to a whole new level by introducing smoosh-ins.

It all seems so obvious now, but Herrell claims to have been the first to offer customers an array of fruits, nuts, candies, and ground-up cookies (Oreos, for example) and candy bars (Heath bars and Reese's cups, to name two) to add to their ice cream. A server would use a metal spatula to smoosh the ice cream and goodies together on a marble countertop. The process was slow—and lines were long—but each custom order was worth the wait. Ice cream lovers burst free from the tyranny of packaged mixtures and reveled in the ability to create their own concoctions. With several dozen ice cream flavors and an equal number of potential smoosh-ins, the possible permutations were mind-boggling.

Perhaps unprepared for the fervor of Massachusetts ice cream lovers, Herrell sold the original Steve's in 1977. Three years later, at practically the moment his non-compete clause expired, Herrell was back in business with his original recipes and a new name. Four shops now operate under the Herrell's brand (see www.herrells.com for locations).

Smoosh-in:

Ice cream pioneer Steve Herrell is credited with launching the now worldwide practice of mashing candy bars and other goodies into already ultra-rich ice cream.

you know you're in
massachusetts when...
...a bridge measures 364.4 smoots (and one ear)

Oliver Reed Smoot Jr. knows a thing or two about standards and measures. Shortly before his retirement at the end of 2005, he served a stint as president of the American National Standards Institute (ANSI), the Washington-based association that helps set guidelines on everything from light bulbs to alphabets used in word processing.

He was probably the only ANSI president who was, himself, a unit of measurement. In 1958 Smoot was the shortest pledge to the Lambda Chi Alpha fraternity at the Massachusetts Institute of Technology. Rather than forcing him to make panty raids to a girls' dorm (of which MIT had none), his fraternity brothers decided to make the other pledges use Smoot to measure and mark the Harvard Bridge, which carries Massachusetts Avenue between Cambridge and Boston. They put a football helmet on the hapless Smoot and rolled him end over end, making a hash mark every 10 smoots. In truly nerdish MIT fashion, the pledges noted that the bridge was exactly 364.4 smoots and one ear long.

The units of measure managed to survive the demolition and reconstruction of the bridge in the 1980s and early 1990s; students still repaint the marks every few years. Road officials even scored the concrete on the sidewalks in 5-foot, 7-inch intervals (the length of one smoot) rather than the conventional 6-foot separations.

Smoot:

In 1958, MIT fraternity pledges measured the Harvard Bridge between Cambridge and Boston by repeatedly laying Oliver Smoot end over end.

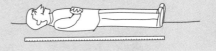

Smoot's son also attended MIT and pledged Lambda Chi Alpha, but he was too tall to serve as a smoot stick. His dad, though, definitely made his mark on the world. Even Boston police use the smoot markers to indicate where accidents have occurred on the bridge. It has been suggested that Smoot found his calling as a freshman and forged a career that measured up.

86

you know you're in
massachusetts when...
... Spenser's on the case

The private sleuth who goes solely by the name of Spenser is Boston's best-known and most enduring gumshoe. Since 1973, when Houghton Mifflin launched *The Godwulf Manuscript,* Spenser has been on the case in more than 30 mystery novels, not to mention three seasons of television programs starring the late Robert Urich as the burly, weight-lifting P.I.

He's the hard-boiled dick who has a sensitive side. Although his creator is a scholar of mystery-and-suspense master Raymond Chandler, Spenser is no Philip Marlowe. He has a life, for one thing. Fans figure that Spenser has everything in perspective—a modest apartment in a great part of town, a manly car that isn't so flashy that punks will steal the headlights, and a girlfriend with brains and beauty (and the incredibly irritating tendency to be right when he's wrong). He has a best friend who would walk through fire for him (and could). And he has a taste for good food, good wine, and the occasional serious literary discussion.

The Spenser code is proof that, as Bob Dylan sang, "To live outside the law, you must be honest." Spenser is often at odds with legality, but he always tries to stay on the side of morality. His shrink girlfriend, Susan Silverman, usually challenges this sense of moral superiority. Spenser nonetheless manages to elucidate the fine points about why it's okay to kill one bad guy and let another one go.

Spenser's real-life doppelganger is his creator, Robert B. Parker, who has not only a first name but also a wife and kids and many friends incapable of handling a semi-automatic weapon. The *Spenser for Hire* TV series is over, and half a dozen Spenser movies have come and gone. But Parker can't seem to kick the Spenser novel habit. "It's a lot like lifting weights," he once told the CBS show *Sunday Morning.* "I love it when I don't have to lift weights. But if I don't do it long enough, then I miss it. You know, I get edgy."

A lot of fans would agree.

Spenser:

Prolific author Robert Parker has written more than 30 mystery novels featuring Boston-based private eye Spenser.

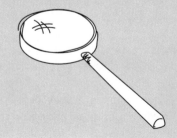

you know you're in

massachusetts when...

... cookies compete and the chips fall where they may

On July 9, 1997, the chocolate chip cookie was named "official cookie of the Commonwealth." Perhaps the Massachusetts Legislature just couldn't say no to the third-graders from Somerset who proposed a bill to promote the cookie that many of them probably carried in their lunch bags.

The cookie certainly has great Massachusetts credentials. It was first baked in the 1930s at the Toll House Inn, located in a 1709 toll house (which had offered food and rest to weary travelers) outside of Whitman. Ruth Wakefield, who ran the lodge's restaurant with her husband, Kenneth, had the inspired idea to chop up a Nestlé's chocolate bar and toss the pieces into a butter cookie recipe that had been around since colonial days.

The cookies were an immediate hit. Ruth soon approached Nestlé and arrived at an arrangement that allowed the company to print her recipe on the package and kept her in a lifetime supply of chocolate. By 1939 Nestlé had introduced its morsels to eliminate the tedious task of chopping the chocolate bar.

But Massachusetts has an even more venerable cookie—the Fig Newton, first manufactured in 1891 by the Kennedy Biscuit Company of Cambridge. Some believe that this healthy mix of fig jam encased in soft dough should have taken the state cookie

title. For one thing, it embodied the engineering prowess that helped make Massachusetts a manufacturing powerhouse in the 19th and early 20th centuries. The cookie was created by a nifty funnel-within-a-funnel apparatus that simultaneously squirted out the jam and enrobed it in the dough. The sweet extrusion was baked and then sliced into cookie-size pieces.

But it's hard to challenge popular taste. Nabisco, the successor to Kennedy Biscuit Company, may tout its Fig Newton as the "official energy snack" of the Ironman Triathlon, but Nestlé insists that the chocolate chip cookie is the "most popular cookie of all time."

As the taste buds go, so goes Massachusetts.

State Cookie:

Two cookies with Massachusetts roots—the Fig Newton, first manufactured in Cambridge, and the toll-house chocolate chip cookie, created near Whitman—vied to represent the Bay State.

you know you're in
massachusetts when...
...a small town looks like an archetypal small town

On the first weekend in December, the town of Stockbridge celebrates the holidays by re-creating the 1967 painting *Home for Christmas*. Better known as "Stockbridge Main Street at Christmas," the idyllic scene was painted by Norman Rockwell (1894–1978), who spent the last 25 years of his life in this southern Berkshires town, which he called "the best of America, the best of New England."

Rolling back the clock 40 years or so is surprisingly easy: Substitute some old sedans and station wagons for today's SUVs and minivans. Rockwell wouldn't feel any time warp if he strolled the well-scrubbed strip of clapboard and brick buildings all in a line, with the Red Lion Inn at the end.

The venerable Red Lion (30 Main Street, 413–298–5545) dates to 1773. It is still the best place to survey the social scene—either by the lobby fireplace in the winter or from one of the coveted rocking chairs on the big front porch when the weather is warm. Rockwell used to eat lunch at the Red Lion every Thursday. It was certainly convenient, given that his first studio was only two doors away, on the upper level of the foursquare redbrick building with gables.

Even if you've never visited before, the little town may look familiar since it was the backdrop for some of Rockwell's most

Stockbridge:

This adopted home of Normal Rockwell was immortalized in the famed illustrator's magazine covers.

memorable vignettes. The setting for the *Saturday Evening Post* cover *Marriage License* is the 1884 former Town Offices on Main Street, now occupied by a branch of Yankee Candle (34 Main Street, 413–298–3004). Elm Street's 1862 firehouse, Hose House No. 1, appeared in *The New American LaFrance Is Here*. Just a few doors down, Shanahan's Elm Street Market (4 Elm Street, 413–298–3634) still serves burgers and ice cream at the soda fountain counter featured in Rockwell's *After the Prom*.

you know you're in
massachusetts when...
...a coaster rates raves

The stakes are literally high in the roller coaster races. It seems that every year another coaster sets records as the tallest or fastest. But top height and speed don't always guarantee top thrill. And thrill is all that really matters, as fans of the Superman Ride of Steel attest.

Installed in 2000 at Six Flags New England in Agawam (better known to longtime amusement park fans as Riverside Park), this steel roller coaster has been rated the "#1 Roller Coaster on the Planet" at least four times by *Park World* magazine, and the ride features on many a coaster fan's top-10 list. Neither a bird nor a plane, the hyperbolic curve rises 208 feet into the sky alongside the Connecticut River. It takes up to 72 passengers on a hair-raising, scream-inducing ride of two and a half minutes.

The longest, highest, and fastest roller coaster in New England (though not in the world), Superman begins with a creaking climb to the top of its first hill, followed by a stomach-wrenching plunge (at a top speed of 77 miles per hour) into a pitch-dark, mist-filled tunnel 13 feet below ground. But one death plunge does not a great coaster make. Superman's strength lies in its continuing twists, turns, loops, and plunges and its perfect positioning for unparalleled views.

The two 36-passenger trains swoop out of the tunnel to a second, lower hill that transitions into a tightly banked turnaround (the G-forces are a sure cure for wrinkles). The pair of humpback hills that follow lift riders off their seats before the train cars spin into two loop-the-loop turns and then plunge into another misty, lightless tunnel.

While other Superman Ride of Steel versions can be found at Six Flags parks elsewhere in the country, the Massachusetts ride has more hills, reaches higher speeds, and is generally considered by enthusiasts to be the finest example of the genre.

Six Flags New England is located at 1623 Main Street, Agawam. For more information, call (413) 786–9300 or visit www .sixflags.com/parks/newengland.

Superman Ride of Steel:

Voted the "#1 Roller Coaster on the Planet" at least four times by *Park World* magazine, the Agawam-based ride draws aficionados from around the globe.

One of the best ways to make new friends at Tanglewood is to remember the corkscrew. Concertgoers at Boston's Symphony Hall try to one-up each other with their dresses and pearls (and their inherited seats). But when the Boston Symphony Orchestra (BSO) heads to the Berkshires countryside for its summer productions at Tanglewood, dinner becomes the measure of sophistication. You are most successful if everyone around you wishes they were dining on your blanket.

The BSO gave its first outdoor performance in the Berkshires in 1936. The following season, the group moved to the swank 210-acre estate of Tanglewood. It was a wet summer, so the orchestra commissioned what is now called the Koussevitzky Music Shed—an open-sided pavilion to shelter the players and any patrons willing to shell out for one of the 5,000 dry seats.

But everyone enjoys the cheap seats (the lawn) before the music begins. Because it is almost impossible to eat a restaurant meal and then get to Tanglewood, park the car, hike to the concert site, and get seated in time to hear the music, patrons bring their own food—and it's rarely cold pizza or Subway sandwiches.

Competitive picnickers begin with the foundation—better a blanket than a bedspread, better a quilt than a blanket, and best of all

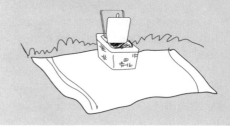

Tanglewood:

The summer home of the Boston Symphony Orchestra is known for superb musicianship and for lavish preconcert picnics on the lawn.

is an Oriental carpet. (This is heavy and requires a family Sherpa or a teenager to lug it.) The fare might include slices of quiche, exquisite noodle salads with slivers of smoked duck, even a silver bowl of caviar on crushed ice. Dessert should be extravagant and chocolate if there's Beethoven on the program, or light and lemon if the BSO is playing Rimsky-Korsakov. Just make it cheese if you're there for Schönberg.

As for the corkscrew—someone nearby will have forgotten to bring one. Concertgoers drinking from screw-tops would die of embarrassment.

Lowell is a rare Massachusetts city, in that it has no colonial past. It was made of whole cloth and came to represent the ups and downs of industrialization.

When Europeans first began touring the United States in significant numbers, two stops were atop all the itineraries: thundering Niagara Falls and the thunderous spinning jennies and looms of Lowell. In the 1840s Lowell represented the utopian ideal of an enlightened industrial city. The textile mill owners would recruit farmers' daughters from the countryside, feed and house them, and pay them fairly enough to let the girls contribute to their families and build a dowry. In return, the mills got a skilled and virtually captive workforce.

It was a high-minded beginning to the American industrial revolution, which had gotten a jump start by pirating the designs of textile machinery invented in England. As long as Lowell's mills had an edge over other American cloth makers, benevolence reigned. But as profit margins were squeezed with new competition, Lowell and its sister mills up and down the Merrimack River adopted a more mercenary relationship with their workforces, which had come to include many immigrants. The upshot was the birth of the American labor movement.

When Lowell collapsed economically in the mid-20th century, the city couldn't afford to tear down its vast redbrick mills. Now many

Textile Mills:

Using pirated technology from Britain, entrepreneurs launched America's industrial revolution in the textile mills of Lowell.

of them—along with 5.6 miles of industrial canals—belong to the Lowell National Historical Park. The park's facilities include an operating weave room of 88 power looms in the former Boott Cotton Mills, "mill girl" boardinghouses, and technical exhibits on the workings of a turbine engine. The interpretive programs do justice both to the extraordinary technological achievements of the Lowell mills and to the proud history of organized labor. Nearly two centuries later, the European tourists are coming again—this time to see how a pioneer mill town honors its past.

The visitor center for the sprawling National Historic Park sits on Merrimack Canal at the corner of Dutton and Market Streets. For more information, call (978) 970–5000 or visit www.nps.gov/lowe.

Good grief.

That's what Charlie Brown would almost surely utter if he stumbled over the giant pumpkins at the annual Topsfield Fair. Sometimes weighing in at more than 1,300 pounds, these orange behemoths bring new meaning to the term *great pumpkin*.

They're also contenders in the Giant Pumpkin Contest, one of the most popular events at the fair. Amid all the distractions of the midway and the grandstand shows, of racing pigs and antique-tractor-pulling competitions, visitors invariably make their way to the Fruit and Vegetable Building. There the big pumpkins rest tenderly on beds of straw—upstaging the displays of 60 other types of vegetables and 21 types of fruit, all of more normal sizes.

The harvest-season extravaganza bills itself as "America's oldest agricultural fair." It debuted in 1820 to give farmers an opportunity to share information on such topics as neat cattle, fat oxen and swine, Indian corn, and manure. It's been an annual event ever since, with the exception of three years during the Civil War and three years during World War II when the fairgrounds remained empty per government decree.

Over the years, the fair has witnessed all sorts of innovations in agricultural practices and animal husbandry—but nothing beats growing giant pumpkins. This seemingly single-minded and meditative pursuit has literally grown more and more competitive since a 433-pound pumpkin took top prize at Topsfield's first Giant Pumpkin Contest in 1984.

Today, that gourd wouldn't even be a contender. So just how big is a 1,300-pound pumpkin? About 15 feet around and 36 inches high.

That's a lot of pie. Even Linus might approve.

Topsfield is in northeast Massachusetts. The 10-day fair is held from late September through early October. Visit www.topsfield fair.org for details.

Topsfield Fair:

The Giant Pumpkin Contest is one of the biggest draws at the Topsfield Fair.

you know you're in
massachusetts when...
...cottages look like doll houses

Praise the Lord! The Trinity Park community in Oak Bluffs on the island of Martha's Vineyard looks more like it was designed by a cabal of confectioners than by an assembly of architects. Roughly 300 cottages adorned with curlicues, scrollwork, balconies, peculiarly pitched eaves, and other Carpenter Gothic fillips survive from the late-19th-century Martha's Vineyard Campmeeting Association.

The neighborhood traces its origins to August 24, 1835, when the first open-air Methodist camp meeting convened for a week of sermons, shared prayer, open confessions, and tearful public conversions. The Martha's Vineyard Methodists saved so many souls that they made the camp meeting an annual event. Roughly 3,000 devout attendees slept in canvas tents (sometimes pitched on wooden platforms) until 1859, when William Lawton of Providence, Rhode Island, constructed the first cottage to spare his family the misery of clammy canvas. Subsequent cottage builders imitated the gingerbread trim of Lawton's cottage, and by the time the conclave reached its peak, it looked like something from the Brothers Grimm.

The camp meeting no longer takes place, but the Trinity Park Methodist Church (1878) still holds services on the grounds, and the open-air, wrought-iron Tabernacle hosts concerts, lectures, high school graduations, and other public activities. On one Wednesday in mid-August, the Tabernacle and many of the cottages are lit with Japanese lanterns for the Grand Illumination, an event that marks the unofficial end of the summer season.

The cottages are private homes, but you can peek inside one at the Cottage Museum, which is staffed by volunteers in the summer and fall. Its light yellow walls, aqua trim, and white scrollwork make it one of the more modestly decorated structures, but it's full of artifacts from the camp meeting days.

The Cottage Museum is located at the corner of Highland Avenue and Trinity Park. For more information on the Campmeeting Association, call (508) 693–0525 or visit www.mvcma.org.

Trinity Park:

The gingerbread cottages of the Martha's Vineyard Campmeeting Association rival each other for colorful paint schemes.

In Dahchestah, they're called "three deckas," but in the rest of urban Massachusetts they're triple-deckers (or "triple deckas"). Until real estate prices climbed to the point where single-family homes sold for the price of a private Caribbean island, the triple-decker was the Rodney Dangerfield of colloquial residential architecture. It got no respect at all.

Part of the disdain no doubt derives from the fact that these altogether serviceable apartment buildings—usually three identical flats stacked on top of each other and linked by interior front and back stairs—were built as immigrant housing. The wood-frame structures went up in a hurry, most of them between 1870 and 1920. Because they were usually freestanding and had windows on all four sides (along with front and back porches or balconies), they were a big step up from the brick tenements built earlier in Boston's North End and adjoining industrial areas like Chelsea.

Entire neighborhoods consist of triple-deckers, especially in South Boston, Dorchester, Somerville, and Winthrop. Family after family of immigrants got a toehold on the new world by purchasing a triple-decker, then renting out two of the flats to relatives freshly arrived from the old country.

Those were the days before condo conversions. Even in cities that once regulated

Triple-Decker:

This staple of late 19th-century eastern Massachusetts residential architecture consists of apartments stacked three high with an interior stairway.

conversion of existing rental housing into condominiums, the three-family, owner-occupied house was generally exempted. (Massachusetts voters overturned these so-called "rent control" laws in a referendum in the 1990s.) Suddenly the three-family house was worth enough that an owner could pay off the mortgage and even make a profit by selling two units.

Just as the triple-decker was once the entry-level housing for new citizens, it has become the entry-level purchase for a first-time home buyer. In real estate–speak, *triple-decker* went from a term of derision to the holy grail of a first home.

you know you're in
massachusetts when...
...a rock star serves as your tour guide

"Let me show you my town," a familiar raspy voice cajoles. "As I love to say, 'Walk This Way.'"

So begins Boston's hippest walking tour. The Talking Street cell phone tour is narrated by Aerosmith lead singer Steven Tyler. Sure, it's a little surprising to find a rock star moonlighting as a tour guide. But as the self-proclaimed "guy with the biggest mouth in the city," Tyler argues that he's a natural to extol Boston's virtues. Memories of his scrambling days in the 1970s have left a soft spot in his heart for the city where the band got its start.

First stop on the "Rebels and Dreamers" tour is the Boston Public Garden, "a garden even a rocker can love." Among the garden's many statues and monuments, Tyler is partial to the often-overlooked Ether Monument, which commemorates the first use of anesthesia at Massachusetts General Hospital in 1846. "Imagine having no painkiller while getting a tooth pulled or a leg amputated," Tyler says before concluding that ether was seen by many as "a gift from the gods."

Tyler also favors the Garden's immensely popular sculpture based on the classic children's book *Make Way for Ducklings*. The father of four appreciates a "book that makes your kid climb into bed at night."

Tyler, Steven:

This rocker, whose band got its start in Boston, narrates the city's Talking Street cell phone tour.

And so it goes, as Tyler puts his unique twist on Beacon Hill, the Granary Burial Ground, Quincy Market, and the Zakim Bridge. The tour has 17 stops in all and takes about two hours, of which cell phone time is about 40 minutes.

A $5.95 fee gives you cell phone access to the tour for 24 hours. Call (617) 262–8687 to pay by credit card and get started. Or place your order for the tour in advance by visiting www.talkingstreet.com.

Despite all of Boston's trendy restaurants and hot young chefs who have been honored by the James Beard Foundation, tradition sometimes trumps innovation. For oysters on the half shell and Wellfleet littlenecks in their own juices, Bostonians and visitors alike crowd around the semicircular bar that's been a fixture at the Union Oyster House since it opened in 1826.

When Union Street was laid out in 1636, it ran right along the waterfront. Although the date of the three-story building clad in brick laid in the old Flemish bond pattern has been lost to history, city records do show that by 1742 a dry goods importer was operating on the site. The building also has Revolutionary credentials: The *Massachusetts Spy* newspaper was published on the upper floor, and the ground floor served as headquarters for the Continental Army's paymaster in 1775. It even had a brief brush with royalty when the Duke of Chartres lived there while in exile, later returning to France and assuming the throne as Louis Philippe.

But the Union Oyster House is most famous in the annals of American gastronomic history as the oldest restaurant in the country in continuous service. The menu has expanded greatly since the original variations on oysters, clams, and scallops. Indeed, many diners prefer the Dover sole and baked cod to the namesake bivalves.

As a young congressman, John F. Kennedy liked to while away Sunday afternoons reading the paper and eating lobster stew. His favorite booth on the second floor—number 18—has a plaque in his honor.

The Union Oyster House is on the Freedom Trail at 41 Union Street, making it possible to stay in historic mode while taking a break and fueling up for the rest of the walk into the North End and Charlestown. For information or a reservation, call (617) 227–2750 or visit www.unionoyster house.com.

Union Oyster House:

When the Union Oyster House opened in 1826, it sat next to the water. It hasn't moved, but the water has.

If it weren't for the "Concord Curmudgeon," Walden Pond would just be another nifty swimming hole—a place for locals to repair to for a refreshing dip on a hot day.

Instead, the pond has been designated a National Historic Landmark and is regarded by many as the birthplace of the conservation movement. Its claim to fame harks back to the roughly two-year stretch from July 1845 to September 1847, when budding writer and philosopher Henry David Thoreau (1817–1862) lived on the edge of the pond in a modest one-room house that he built himself. With few distractions, Thoreau studied the details of the natural world and mused on matters of natural philosophy. Though he rarely wrote a sentence with fewer than 50 words, snippets of his ideas have become aphorisms quoted everywhere from greeting cards to book dedications. Thoreau's pond-side idyll became the basis for his most famous book, *Walden; or, Life in the Woods*, published in 1854.

Many visitors make a pilgrimage to a replica of Thoreau's home, where a bronze statue of the author stands out front. Ralph Waldo Emerson, Thoreau's friend and mentor, owned the land that Thoreau built on, and he sold the original cottage after Thoreau left in 1847. It was moved elsewhere in Concord to store grain before being dismantled in 1868.

Thoreau would have liked the idea that his cabin was put to practical use—and the fact that the park continues to serve as an escape from the densely populated towns nearby. The 102-foot-deep glacial kettle pond attracts swimmers and fishermen alike. The 400-acre reservation has trails for quiet, woodsy contemplation. But don't bring your dog along for company; canines are not allowed.

The pond is so popular that visitors are limited to 1,000 at a time. For more information, call the Walden Pond State Reservation at (978) 369–3254 or visit www.mass.gov/dcr/parks/northeast/wldn.htm. The Visitors Center is at 915 Walden Street in Concord. Rangers lead walks and conduct other educational programs year-round.

Walden Pond:

Henry David Thoreau lived for more than two years in a one-room home at the pond, an experience chronicled in his book *Walden; or, Life in the Woods*.

you know you're in
massachusetts when...
... pirate loot comes ashore

Cannon and cannon balls, pistols and a cutlass, more than 3,000 silver coins minted by the Spanish empire in Mexico and Peru, a leather shoe, a silk stocking, three cuff links, and a candlesnuffer—all these items only hint at the riches aboard the pirate ship *Whydah* when it sank in a raging storm off Marconi Beach in Wellfleet on April 26, 1717.

In 1984 underwater explorer Barry Clifford located the *Whydah*—no small feat, given that the 300-ton galley was buried beneath 10 feet of sand in 20 feet of water. Over the next decade Clifford and his crew recovered more than 100,000 artifacts. The value of this treasure, which had been plundered by the pirate Black Sam Bellamy from more than 50 ships, is a matter of great speculation, but Clifford has opted to keep the collection intact rather than sell it. The object he prizes most highly is an 18-inch bell that came to the surface in 1985. Inscribed THE WHYDAH GALLEY 1716, it confirmed that the Cape Cod wreck is the first pirate ship to be identified and salvaged.

Some of the loot is on display in the Whydah Pirate Museum on MacMillan Wharf in Provincetown, where exhibits also shed the light of historic fact on the often-romanticized pirate lifestyle. The same building houses the Expedition Whydah Sea Lab and Learning Center, the base for ongoing excavations at the *Whydah* site. Lucky

Whydah:

Black Sam Bellamy's pirate ship foundered off Cape Cod in 1717, but Barry Clifford found the wreck 267 years later and displays some of the cargo in a Provincetown museum.

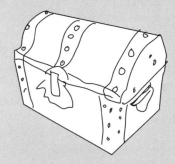

visitors may even be on hand when one of the recovery vessels returns with a new treasure trove.

If the *Whydah* recovery has inspired your own dreams of pirate treasure, be advised that Cape Cod's shifting shoals and treacherous currents have claimed many a vessel. Clifford has estimated that there are about 3,000 shipwrecks lying in the offshore sands.

The Whydah Pirate Museum is open from spring through fall. For information, call (508) 487–8899 or visit www.whydah.com.

In June 2005 a 9-foot-tall bronze statue of Samantha Stephens sitting sidesaddle on a broom was unveiled in downtown Salem. The homage to the "good witch" of the television show *Bewitched* brings to mind Salem's darker past.

In 1692 the citizens succumbed to hysteria and executed 20 people as witches, an episode that left a permanent blot on the early history of the colonies. Salem managed to move on and become a prosperous trading port in the 18th and 19th centuries. You'd think that the city might hope that its period of shame would just fade away. No such luck.

The city has an outstanding art museum, a National Historic Park focused on its glory days in the age of sailing, and the House of Seven Gables, which was made famous by author Nathaniel Hawthorne. But the largest number of visitors gravitate to the Salem Witch Museum for a multimedia presentation on the witch trials and an exhibit that explores popular perceptions of witchcraft through the ages. The city's own quiet memorial to the tragic episode was dedicated on the 300th anniversary and is located on Liberty Street.

Things really heat up in October, when the city presents Salem's Haunted Happenings. Three weeks of events include candlelit tours, haunted houses, a supernatural stroll, scary tales, and even a haunted car wash.

Witch Trials:

Apparently unrepentant for having executed 20 people as witches in 1692, Salem continues to trade on its dark past.

Salem's modern-day practitioners of the ancient arts associated with witchcraft counter with a month-long Psychic Fair and Witchcraft Expo. In addition to having their futures divined through astrology or tarot or palm readings, visitors might want to learn how to construct a witch's broom or concoct a love potion. The event culminates with the Official Salem Witches Ball, which purports to attract witches from around the world. Organizers are mum on their mode of transportation.

The Salem Witch Museum is on Washington Square. For more information, call (978) 744–1692 or visit www.salemwitchmuseum.org. For information on the October events, visit www.hauntedhappenings.org or www.festivalofthedead.com.

You could think of the village of Woods Hole as the place where Mr. Wizard meets L. L. Bean, a town where science geeks have a good tan and wear flip-flops. Its location between Nantucket Sound and Buzzards Bay made it a fine fishing port when it was settled in the 17th century. But by 1871, when the precursor of the National Marine Fisheries Service established its first research station in Woods Hole, fishing was waning. So the village evolved as one of the world's preeminent marine science communities.

The free Fisheries Service aquarium is a nifty place to get a look at dinner on the fin, so to speak, since it focuses on commercially important species found off the New England coast. A few touch tanks are set low to the ground to encourage youngsters to handle such sturdy creatures as whelks, starfish, and lobsters (with their claws clamped shut, of course).

Other research institutions followed the Fisheries' lead. Over at the Marine Biological Laboratory (MBL), scientists also often handle sturdy sea creatures, most notably horseshoe crabs. These ancient arthropods have blue, copper-based blood used in cancer research. The MBL has just a few exhibits for the public; most of the research involves the intersection of marine biology and medicine.

Woods Hole Oceanographic Institution (WHOI) exemplifies the Indiana Jones

scientist-adventurer side of Woods Hole, boldly going to the last frontiers of inner space—the ocean depths. The main research campus is outside town, but a fascinating exhibit center includes a model submersible that visitors can crawl in. Films show WHOI's underwater exploration of the *Titanic* and of the spooky, otherworldly regions of hydrothermal vents, where rifts in the ocean floor pump out hot chemical plumes to support an ecosystem as diverse as a rain forest.

The National Marine Fisheries Service Aquarium is on Albatross Street. For more information, call (508) 495–2001 or visit aquarium.nefsc.noaa.gov. The WHOI Exhibit Center is at 15 Market Street. For information, call (508) 457–2000, ext. 2252 or 2663, or visit www.whoi.edu.

Woods Hole:

Three preeminent ocean-science centers call this Cape Cod village home.

index

a

Adams, John, 76
Adams, John Quincy, 76
Aquinnah cliffs, 37

b

Basketball Hall of Fame, 2
Battleship Cove, 3
battles of Lexington and Concord, 4
Berklee College of Music, 6
Big Chair, 7
Borden, Lizzie, 8
Boston accent, 9
Boston Brahmin, 10
Boston Bruins, 11
Boston Celtics, 12
Boston cream pie, 13
Boston Harbor Light, 14
Boston Marathon, 15
Boston Pops, 38, 91
Boston Red Sox, 16
Bridge of Flowers, 17
Brimfield, 18
Brownies, 19

c

Cape Cod Baseball League, 20
Cape Cod National Seashore, 5
Cape Cod parcels, 21
Charlie Card, 22
Chinatown, 23
chowder, clam, 24
CITGO sign, 25
Click and Clack, 26
cottages, 27
cranberries, 28

d

Day of Mourning, National, 29
diners, 30

Dr. Seuss, 31

e

Emerald Necklace, 32
Evacuation Day, 33

f

Feast of the Blessed Sacrament, 34
Filene's Basement, 35
First Night, 36
fossils, 37
Fourth of July, 38
frappe, 39
Freedom Trail, 40
fried clams, 41

g

Gardner Museum, 42
gawkablocka, 43
glacial geology, 44
glass flowers, 45
Guthrie, Arlo, 46

h

Harvard Yard, 47
Head of the Charles Regatta, 48
heart health, 49
heirloom apples, 50
Higgins Armory Museum, 51
Hilltop Steak House, 52
Herrell, Steve, 85

i

Indian motorcycle, 53
Irish, 54

j

Jacob's Pillow, 55
Jimmy Fund, 56

k

Kennedy family, 57

l

L Street Brownies, 19
Le Grand David, 58
Leonard P. Zakim Bunker Hill Bridge, 59
Lilac Sunday, 60

m

Man at the Wheel, The, 61
Mapparium, 62
Martha's Vineyard Campmeeting
    Association, 94
Massachusetts Museum of Contemporary
    Art, 63
Mayflower Compact, 64
Moby-Dick, 65
Mohawk Trail, 66
Motif No. 1, 67
Mount Greylock, 68
Museum of Fine Arts, 69

n

NECCO, 70
New England Patriots, 71
North End festivals, 72

p

Parker, Robert B., 87
Plimoth Plantation, 73
Provincetown, 74

q

Quabbin, 75
Quincy, 76

r

reformers, 77
rotary, 78

s

Sacred Cod, 79
Saint-Gaudens, Augustus, 82
Salem, 100
Samuel Adams, 80
scrod, 81
Shaw Memorial, 82
Siasconset, 83
Singing Beach, 84
smoosh-in, 85
smoot, 86
Spenser, 87
state cookie, 88
Stockbridge, 89
Superman Ride of Steel, 90

t

Tanglewood, 91
textile mills, 92
Thoreau, Henry David, 98
Topsfield Fair, 93
Trinity Park, 94
triple-decker, 95
Tyler, Steven, 96

u

Union Oyster House, 97

w

Walden Pond, 98
Whydah, 99
witch trials, 100
Woods Hole, 101

z

ZIP code, Harvard, 1

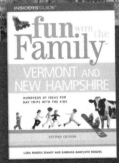

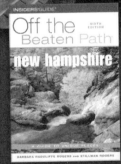